D1063496

The Bible
in STAINED GLASS

First published in the UK
by Bible Society
Stonehill Green, Westlea
Swindon SN5 7DG

ISBN 0564 071 358

First published in the USA
by Morehouse Publishing
Editorial office
871 Ethan Allen Highway
Ridgefield, CT 06877
Corporate office
P.O. Box 1321
Harrisburg, PA 17105

ISBN 0 8192 1552 X

Designed and created by
Three's Company
12 Flitcroft Street
London WC2H 8DJ

Designer: Peter Wyart

Worldwide co-edition organised and produced by
Angus Hudson Ltd
Concorde House,
Grenville Place,
Mill Hill,
London NW7 3SA

Printed in Singapore

The Bible in STAINED GLASS

Photographs by Sonia Halliday and Laura Lushington
Descriptive text by Laura Lushington

EDITED BY DR TIM DOWLEY

The Windows

OLD TESTAMENT

NEW TESTAMENT

Foreword

By Peter Gibson
Secretary/Superintendent of the York Glazier's Trust

The art and craft of stained glass has enriched cathedrals, parish churches and countless other ecclesiastical and secular buildings for more than one thousand years. Few journeys can be more rewarding than to enter any building containing figurative stained glass and to trace in its storied windows their unfolding religious or secular themes.

In the Middle Ages the windows were a visual teaching aid, where biblical stories were re-enacted for the onlooker in a feast of glorious coloured glass and medieval design. Centuries later, in the twentieth century, we have inherited many of these surviving treasures of glass that are a witness to the skills of the medieval craftsmen.

As one who has had the great privilege of caring for stained glass all my life, I have indeed been fortunate to have had the constant daily pleasure of seeing fascinating details of glass painting of all ages at eye level – a rare and unforgettable experience. Readers of *The Bible in Stained Glass* will be able to enjoy this same memorable experience. Not only will they be able to share in the history of the craft, but the superb illustrations are accompanied by the appropriate biblical texts which have inspired glass painters, artists and craftsmen throughout the ages.

I hope and pray that these Bible stories in stained glass will serve not only as an inspiration to all readers, but as a constant testimony to the Glory of God in whom and by whom all things were created.

Peter Gibson

Introduction

Beginnings

It is interesting to realise that stained glass did not exist before Christian times; the art of stained glass is essentially a Christian art. In Christian churches the windows became a means not only of illuminating a building, but also of communicating visually Bible stories, and thus Christian truth.

We cannot date with any great accuracy the first appearance of stained glass windows. However, it seems probable that this craft evolved from the artistic use of mosaics and enamel work to decorate early Christian churches. Possibly the first stained-glass craftsmen borrowed their techniques from the goldsmith, who, in making jewellery and ornaments, bent strips of gold around precious gems to hold them together. With coloured glass becoming more readily available, it became possible to think of making small coloured windows, binding the glass together with malleable lead in a similar manner to the goldsmith.

Other innovations followed. For instance, it was discovered that iron filings mixed with powdered glass could be painted onto glass to represent the detail required in a design, and then made permanent by firing the glass to just short of its boiling point.

Although there are tantalising glimpses of earlier coloured glass windows, the first firm evidence we have is of a stained glass figural window at Jarrow, north-east England, dating from some time between 685 – 800A.D. There also survive some fragments from Lorsch Abbey, Germany, dating from the ninth or tenth century A.D. These fragments were only discovered during excavations in 1932. Other early stained glass windows include a head of Christ from Wissembourg, Alsace, France and five 'prophet' windows in Augsburg Cathedral, Germany.

Gothic churches

Whilst the earliest stained glass was designed for Romanesque churches, with their characteristic single semi-circular-headed windows, it was with the coming of the Gothic style of architecture, with its vast expanses of glazing, that stained glass truly came into its own. The great Gothic cathedrals of medieval Western Europe offered vast potential to the stained-glass craftsman. As the classic form of the Gothic cathedral-church developed, it offered to the glazier the great rose window above the western entrance; a series of glazed aisles and galleries in the nave; the transepts, each with their own windows; and finally the high east windows in the choir.

Joseph in the Pit; Chartres Cathedral.

Detail of Noah building the ark; Chartres Cathedral, France.

As the master-masons extended their artistic skills and technical knowledge, their ever more complex systems of buttressing and vaulting made possible increasingly expansive areas of stained glass, with the resulting magical effects of constantly changing light and colour. The glazier's art in many ways reached its peak in the High Middle Ages; later developments in architecture, and shifts in the spirit of the age, meant there was a decreasing demand for the skill and ingenuity of the stained glass craftsman.

However, twentieth-century advances in building technology, and particularly the development of reinforced concrete for building purposes, have meant that today once more the stained glass artist can be called on to cover huge areas which are supported by elegantly slim steel or concrete structures.

Glass and light

The uniqueness of stained glass as an artistic medium is that it relies for its effect entirely on the impact of natural light upon it. The artist deals not only in the coloured glass itself, but also in the effects that natural light will have as it passes through the glass. It is as if the craftsman is actually painting with light.

The Bible in stained glass

Naturally, the main theme of stained glass in churches, from the earliest examples until today, has been biblical. Although there are many exceptions, such as the depiction of saints and martyrs, the glorification of local magnates, and memorials to relations or the war-dead, the great mass of ecclesiastical stained glass draws on the Old and New Testaments for its subject matter.

But there is no haphazard selection of themes in church glass. Although stained glass was undoubtedly valued for its contribution to the beauty, sanctity and richness of a church building, it was also employed as an effective means of communication, and a comprehensible means of instruction to the faithful worshippers.

It should never be forgotten that the great mass of medieval people would have been illiterate. Moreover, the Latin services of the church would have been almost totally incomprehensible to them. They would rely on catching a familiar Latin word to tell them that they had reached a particular point in the service. Amidst such ignorance and illiteracy, all the more place for the use of the pictorial language of the stained glass window for instructing people in Christian faith and practice.

Thus the scriptural incidents, characters and themes illustrated in medieval stained glass are normally carefully selected for the moral or doctrinal teaching they might convey. Stories such as the destruction of Sodom, the murder of Abel, and the Great Flood served as dreadful warnings. Other windows portrayed the Old Testament prophets, and showed how they foretold Christ's birth, mission and death. Another common theme in medieval glass was the 'Jesse tree', depicting graphically the genealogy of King David's line, from his father Jesse, through the kings of Judah down eventually to Jesus Christ, 'Great David's greater Son'.

The grotesque

There is also a strong tradition in medieval stained glass of the grotesque and frightening; portrayals of the Last Judgment and the terrors of Hell, to warn the erring of the danger of their ways. The artists seem particularly to have enjoyed the opportunity to exercise their imagination for strange and weird creatures.

In addition to these relatively

Gabriel Loire working in his studio near Chartres on a cartoon for a window in Coignières Church, France.

The thirteenth-century North Rose Window, Notre Dame, Paris, France.

Gabriel Loire at work on the cartoon for 'Christ's Charge to Peter'.

The Passion and Apocalypse windows, Bourges Cathedral, France.

straightforward approaches, stained glass also often reflected the more complex strands of medieval biblical interpretation. There is a tradition of portraying types and antitypes; that is, Old Testament incidents (types) supposed to prefigure New Testament events (antitypes). For instance, Jonah's swallowing by, and later deliverance from, the great fish is matched with an illustration of Christ's entombment in the earth and subsequent resurrection. Similarly, the Queen of Sheba's visit to King Solomon to present rich gifts is represented as prefiguring the visit of the Wise Men from the East bearing their gifts of gold, frankincense and myrrh for the baby Jesus.

A well-known and accomplished example of types and antitypes is the Poor Man's Bible windows in Canterbury Cathedral, Kent. The popular name for these windows itself reflects the way that windows served the poor and illiterate as some sort of graphic Scripture.

The great feasts and festivals of the church year figured large in medieval life, and were also widely reflected in the subject matter of stained glass. Such windows helped explain the significance of the respective festival, and doubtless became something of a focus of attention when that particular festival came round. Such festivals as Christmas, Easter, the Annunciation and Palm Sunday were frequently celebrated in stained glass, and illustrated by incidents from the gospel narrative concerning the nativity, the passion, the virgin Mary etc.

Design sources

But we should not imagine that the medieval stained glass artist relied solely on his own visual imagination for his designs. Much of his visual material was drawn from common sources, particularly the richly-decorated illuminated manuscripts which were a prized feature of medieval monasteries. Certainly many designs seem to have been copied from such manuscript sources; indeed, some windows are so similar to known miniature designs on paper that it even seems possible that the same craftsman may have been responsible for both illustrations.

In drawing up his design, the stained glass artist would use sketches drawn out on parchment. He would only have a limited number of such patterns; hence the frequently-observed repetition of figures, perhaps varied by being reversed left-to-right or having their gender changed! With the introduction of paper to the West, it became practical to develop a wider range of patterns – and to pass them on from generation to generation.

The medieval artist had no notion of originality being a merit in and of itself; indeed, continuity and tradition were positively valued by medieval society. Moreover, with the sheer amount of work to be accomplished, the medieval stained glass artist seems rather to have put a premium on speed of execution and useful shortcuts.

Visual aids

Thus the stained glass window – to the modern tourist above all an object of beauty and mystery – also represented to the medieval Christian a vital visual communication of Christian truth. In this way the church fabric itself was drawn to the service of Christian teaching.

Nevertheless, in their quest to depict Bible stories and characters graphically and colourfully, in the best instances the craftsmen have transcended their art and produced works which contribute to the overall mystery and grandeur of the medieval cathedral and church, and to the worship of God.

Dr Tim Dowley

CONTENTS

THE OLD TESTAMENT

God, the designer of the universe
Panel from the fifteenth-century Creation Window, south choir aisle, St Anne's Chapel, Great Malvern Priory, Worcestershire, England.

CREATION

IN the beginning God created the heaven and the earth. And the earth was without form, and void; and darkness was upon the face of the deep. And the Spirit of God moved upon the face of the waters. And God said, Let there be light: and there was light. And God saw the light, that it was good: and God divided the light from the darkness. And God called the light Day, and the darkness he called Night. And the evening and the morning were the first day.

And God said, Let there be a firmament in the midst of the waters, and let it divide the waters from the waters. And God made the firmament, and divided the waters which were under the firmament from the waters which were above the firmament: and it was so. And God called the firmament Heaven. And the evening and the morning were the second day.

And God said, Let the waters under the heaven be gathered together unto one place, and let the dry land appear: and it was so. And God called the dry land Earth; and the gathering together of the waters called he Seas: and God saw that it was good.

GENESIS
Chapter 1:1–10

The creation of Eve
Fourteenth-century German panel from the Church of St Etienne, Mulhouse, Alsace, France.

God is represented in the act of creation, lifting by one hand the fully-adult Eve, who has long, fair hair, from the rib-cage of the sleeping Adam. In the lower right-hand corner is a sprig or branch, possibly to symbolize life. God's right hand is raised as if blessing his new creation.

Creation and the Fall
Panels from the Creation Window, ambulatory, St Florentin Church, Burgundy, France; 1525.

God the Creator is here depicted wearing a pope's triple tiara and jewelled cope. This window, with its four panels picturing the Creation and four picturing the Fall, is believed to originate from the same school of craftsmen as the Creation Window in La Madeleine, Troyes.

GENESIS
Chapter 3:1–24

THE SERPENT DECEIVES EVE

NOW the serpent was more subtil than any beast of the field which the LORD God had made. And he said unto the woman, Yea, hath God said, Ye shall not eat of every tree of the garden? And the woman said unto the serpent, We may eat of the fruit of the trees of the garden: But of the fruit of the tree which is in the midst of the garden, God hath said, Ye shall not eat of it, neither shall ye touch it, lest ye die. And the serpent said unto the woman, Ye shall not surely die: For God doth know that in the day ye eat thereof, then your eyes shall be opened, and ye shall be as gods, knowing good and evil. And when the woman saw that the tree was good for food, and that it was pleasant to the eyes, and a tree to be desired to make one wise, she took of the fruit thereof, and did eat, and gave also unto her husband with her; and he did eat. And the eyes of them both were opened, and they knew that they were naked; and they sewed fig leaves together, and made themselves aprons. And they heard the voice of the LORD God walking in the garden in the cool of the day: and Adam and his wife hid themselves from the presence of the LORD God amongst the trees of the garden. And the LORD God called unto Adam, and said unto him, Where art thou? And he said, I heard thy voice in the garden, and I was afraid, because I was naked; and I hid myself. And he said, Who told thee that thou wast naked? Hast thou eaten of the tree, whereof I commanded thee

that thou shouldest not eat? And the man said, The woman whom thou gavest to be with me, she gave me of the tree, and I did eat. And the LORD God said unto the woman, What is this that thou hast done? And the woman said, The serpent beguiled me, and I did eat. And the LORD God said unto the serpent, Because thou hast done this, thou art cursed above all cattle, and above every beast of the field; upon thy belly shalt thou go, and dust shalt thou eat all the days of thy life: And I will put enmity between thee and the woman, and between thy seed and her seed; it shall bruise thy head, and thou shalt bruise his heel. Unto the woman he said, I will greatly multiply thy sorrow and thy conception; in sorrow thou shalt bring forth children; and thy desire shall be to thy husband, and he shall rule over thee. And unto Adam he said, Because thou hast hearkened unto the voice of thy wife, and hast eaten of the tree, of which I commanded thee, saying, Thou shalt not eat of it: cursed is the ground for thy sake; in sorrow shalt thou eat of it all the days of thy life; Thorns also and thistles shall it bring forth to thee; and thou shalt eat the herb of the field; In the sweat of thy face shalt thou eat bread, till thou return unto the ground; for out of it wast thou taken: for dust thou art, and unto dust shalt thou return. And Adam called his wife's name Eve; because she was the mother of all living. Unto Adam also and to his wife did the LORD God make coats of skins, and clothed them.

And the LORD God said, Behold, the man is become as one of us, to know good and evil: and now, lest he put forth his hand, and take also of the tree of life, and eat, and live for ever: Therefore the LORD God sent him forth from the garden of Eden, to till the ground from whence he was taken. So he drove out the man; and he placed at the east of the garden of Eden Cherubims, and a flaming sword which turned every way, to keep the way of the tree of life.

Adam delving
Fifteenth-century panel from East Window, Church of St Mary Magdalene, Mulbarton, Norfolk, England.

This is a common subject in stained glass. Here, Adam is shown working barefoot; a very painful way of digging with a spade of this type. (African tribes refused this implement, preferring their own hoe.) Some of the sketchy plants in the background lie sideways, probably to fit the shape of the glass. All the glass in the East Window originally belonged to Martham Church, Norfolk.

Adam constructs his house
Panel from the sixteenth-century Creation Window, La Madeleine, Troyes, Aube, France.

Although at first sight Adam appears to be building a timber-frame house, in fact the wood may be simply the scaffolding for the construction of a stone house; the elaborate bevelled and grooved stone arch possibly represents the beginnings of this building. In any event, Eve is already seated with her children in the lower part of the house, the wall of which is formed of withies woven between wooden stakes. The children have probably been given contrasting features and skin-colourings to signify the origins of different racial types. This window is similar in style to the Creation Window at St Florentin, and may originate from the same school of craftsmen.

CAIN AND ABEL

AND Adam knew Eve his wife; and she conceived, and bare Cain, and said, I have gotten a man from the LORD. And she again bare his brother Abel. And Abel was a keeper of sheep, but Cain was a tiller of the ground. And in process of time it came to pass, that Cain brought of the fruit of the ground an offering unto the LORD. And Abel, he also brought of the firstlings of his flock and of the fat thereof. And the LORD had respect unto Abel and to his offering: But unto Cain and to his offering he had not respect. And Cain was very wroth, and his countenance fell. And the LORD said unto Cain, Why art thou wroth? and why is thy countenance fallen? If thou doest well, shalt thou not be accepted? and if thou doest not well, sin lieth at the door. And unto thee shall be his desire, and thou shalt rule over him. And Cain talked with Abel his brother: and it came to pass, when they were in the field, that Cain rose up against Abel his brother, and slew him.

And the LORD said unto Cain, Where is Abel thy brother? And he said, I know not: Am I my brother's keeper?

GENESIS
Chapter 4:1–9

Cain murders Abel
Fifteenth-century panel by Hans Acker, Besserer Chapel, Ulm Cathedral, Germany.

Cain is shown looking slyly to his left, as if wary of unseen witnesses, as he embeds his adze in his brother Abel's shoulder. *Top left*, Cain, hiding the blade of his murderous weapon behind his back, is admonished by God.

Cain's and Abel's sacrifices
Ford Madox Brown, 1866–70; All Saints' Church, Middleton Cheney, Northamptonshire, England.

Ford Madox Brown, though never a member of the Pre-Raphaelite Brotherhood of Victorian painters, was much influenced by their style and precepts. He belonged to William Morris' firm of stained glass manufacturers from 1861-74. Here the artist has contrasted Cain and Abel as strongly as possible; in physique, facial features, costume and in stance. Cain is muscular, his face full of bitterness and jealousy; Abel is depicted gazing heavenward in humble devotion.

NOAH'S ARK

THESE are the generations of Noah: Noah was a just man and perfect in his generations, and Noah walked with God. And Noah begat three sons, Shem, Ham, and Japheth. The earth also was corrupt before God, and the earth was filled with violence. And God looked upon the earth, and, behold, it was corrupt; for all flesh had corrupted his way upon the earth. And God said unto Noah, The end of all flesh is come before me; for the earth is filled with violence through them; and, behold, I will destroy them with the earth.

Make thee an ark of gopher wood; rooms shalt thou make in the ark, and shalt pitch it within and without with pitch. And this is the fashion which thou shalt make it of: The length of the ark shall be three hundred cubits, the breadth of it fifty cubits, and the height of it thirty cubits. A window shalt thou make to the ark, and in a cubit shalt thou finish it above; and the door of the ark shalt thou set in the side thereof; with lower, second, and third stories shalt thou make it. And, behold, I, even I, do bring a flood of waters upon the earth, to destroy all flesh, wherein is the breath of life, from under heaven; and every thing that is in the earth shall die. But with thee will I establish my covenant; and thou shalt come into the ark, thou, and thy sons, and thy wife, and thy sons' wives with thee. And of every living thing of all flesh, two of every sort shalt thou bring into the ark, to keep them alive with thee; they shall be male and female. Of fowls after their kind, and of cattle after their kind, of every creeping thing of the earth after his kind, two of every sort shall come unto thee, to keep them alive. And take thou unto thee of all food that is eaten, and thou shalt gather it to thee; and it shall be for food for thee, and for them. Thus did Noah; according to all that God commanded him, so did he.

And the LORD said unto Noah, Come thou and all thy house into the ark; for thee have I seen righteous before me in this generation. Of every clean beast thou shalt take to thee by sevens, the male and his female: and of beasts that are not clean by two, the male and his female. Of fowls also of the air by sevens, the male and the female; to keep seed alive upon the face of all the earth. For yet seven days, and I will cause it to rain upon the earth forty days and forty nights; and every living substance that I have made will I destroy from off the face of the earth. And Noah did according unto all that the LORD commanded him. And Noah was six hundred years old when the flood of waters was upon the earth.

And Noah went in, and his sons, and his wife, and his sons' wives with him, into the ark, because of the waters of the flood. Of clean beasts, and of beasts that are not clean, and of fowls, and of every thing that creepeth upon the earth, There went in two and two unto Noah into the ark, the male and the female, as God had commanded Noah. And it came to pass after seven days, that the waters of the flood were upon the earth.

In the six hundredth year of Noah's life, in the second month, the seventeenth day of the month, the same day were all the fountains of the great deep broken up, and the windows of heaven were opened. And the rain was upon the earth forty days and forty nights.

GENESIS
Chapter 6:9–22; 7:1–12

The dove returns to the ark
Detail from the thirteenth-century East Window, South Choir Aisle, Lincoln Cathedral, England.

Noah's fingers are depicted as fine and very long, to draw attention to the significance of the return of the dove, which bears in its beak a leafy twig. Further evidence that the waters have receded is provided by the appearance of a tree near the ark's prow. The bright red triangular panel behind Noah's head may be a 'patch' inserted at a later date.

Noah's Ark
Window by Georg Meistermann in the Marienkirche, Kalk, Cologne, Germany; 1966.

THE TOWER OF BABEL

AND the whole earth was of one language, and of one speech. And it came to pass, as they journeyed from the east, that they found a plain in the land of Shinar; and they dwelt there. And they said one to another, Go to, let us make brick, and burn them throughly. And they had brick for stone, and slime had they for morter. And they said, Go to, let us build us a city and a tower, whose top may reach unto heaven; and let us make us a name, lest we be scattered abroad upon the face of the whole earth. And the LORD came down to see the city and the tower, which the children of men builded. And the LORD said, Behold, the people is one, and they have all one language; and this they begin to do: and now nothing will be restrained from them, which they have imagined to do. Go to, let us go down, and there confound their language, that they may not understand one another's speech. So the LORD scattered them abroad from thence upon the face of all the earth: and they left off to build the city. Therefore is the name of it called Babel; because the LORD did there confound the language of all the earth: and from thence did the LORD scatter them abroad upon the face of all the earth.

GENESIS
Chapter 11:1–9

Building the Tower of Babel
Fourteenth-century German panel, Church of St Etienne, Mulhouse, Alsace, France.

The artist has given the four builders differing heights, features, costumes and skin colouring to show their different races. God is depicted as a venerable man, with white hair, beard and moustache, penetrating eyes, and his mouth open as if in speech. The builders are using medieval tools such as a masonry hammer, wooden mallet and hod.

The Tower of Babel
Seventeenth-century Dutch roundel, St Mary's Church, Bishopsbourne, Kent, England.

Both naked and clothed figures are depicted working together; the naked people are probably slaves. The clothed figures are pictured in seventeenth-century costume, and include two women carrying bricks, dressed in best bib and tucker (i.e. apron top and skirt-protector). The window gives ample evidence about contemporary masonry and building methods.

THE LORD APPEARS TO ABRAHAM

AND when Abram was ninety years old and nine, the LORD appeared to Abram, and said unto him, I am the Almighty God; walk before me, and be thou perfect. And I will make my covenant between me and thee, and will multiply thee exceedingly. And Abram fell on his face: and God talked with him, saying, As for me, behold, my covenant is with thee, and thou shalt be a father of many nations. Neither shall thy name any more be called Abram, but thy name shall be Abraham; for a father of many nations have I made thee. And I will make thee exceeding fruitful, and I will make nations of thee, and kings shall come out of thee. And I will establish my covenant between me and thee and thy seed after thee in their generations for an everlasting covenant, to be a God unto thee, and to thy seed after thee. And I will give unto thee, and to thy seed after thee, the land wherein thou art a stranger, all the land of Canaan, for an everlasting possession; and I will be their God.

And God said unto Abraham, As for Sarai thy wife, thou shalt not call her name Sarai, but Sarah shall her name be. And I will bless her, and give thee a son also of her: yea, I will bless her, and she shall be a mother of nations; kings of people shall be of her. Then Abraham fell upon his face, and laughed, and said in his heart, Shall a child be born unto him that is an hundred years old? and shall Sarah, that is ninety years old, bear? And Abraham said unto God, O that Ishmael might live before thee! And God said, Sarah thy wife shall bear thee a son indeed; and thou shalt call his name Isaac: and I will establish my covenant with him for an everlasting covenant, and with his seed after him.

GENESIS
Chapter 17:1–8; 15–19

God's covenant with Abraham
Fifteenth-century window in the South Choir Aisle, St Anne's Chapel, Great Malvern Priory Church, Worcestershire, England.

Abraham is depicted dressed in a jewel-bordered robe, to denote his exalted rank. The figure of God is robed in scarlet. Three trees and some of the flora are painted with silver nitrate on white glass; when fired this produces a weather-resistant lemon-yellow or orange. It has been suggested that this window was painted by the craftsman who also created the St William Window in York Minster.

Lot's wife looks back
From the early thirteenth-century 'Poor Man's Bible Window', North Choir Aisle, Canterbury Cathedral, Kent, England.

Two angels attempt to encourage Lot's little party on their way. Lot's reluctance to leave Sodom is shown by the way he leans back; his wife, her head turned to look back at the ruins of burning Sodom, is already rigid and white – half-transformed to a pillar of salt.

dñs apparuit

ABRAHAM AND ISAAC

AND Abraham rose up early in the morning, and saddled his ass, and took two of his young men with him, and Isaac his son, and clave the wood for the burnt offering, and rose up, and went unto the place of which God had told him. Then on the third day Abraham lifted up his eyes, and saw the place afar off. And Abraham said unto his young men, Abide ye here with the ass; and I and the lad will go yonder and worship, and come again to you. And Abraham took the wood of the burnt offering, and laid it upon Isaac his son; and he took the fire in his hand, and a knife; and they went both of them together. And Isaac spake unto Abraham his father, and said, My father: and he said, Here am I, my son. And he said, Behold the fire and the wood: but where is the lamb for a burnt offering? And Abraham said, My son, God will provide himself a lamb for a burnt offering: so they went both of them together. And they came to the place which God had told him of; and Abraham built an altar there, and laid the wood in order, and bound Isaac his son, and laid him on the altar upon the wood. And Abraham stretched forth his hand, and took the knife to slay his son. And the angel of the LORD called unto him out of heaven, and said, Abraham, Abraham: and he said, Here am I. And he said, Lay not thine hand upon the lad, neither do thou any thing unto him: for now I know that thou fearest God, seeing thou hast not withheld thy son, thine only son from me. And Abraham lifted up his eyes, and looked, and behold behind him a ram caught in a thicket by his horns: and Abraham went and took the ram, and offered him up for a burnt offering in the stead of his son.

GENESIS
Chapter 22:3–13

Abraham
Panel from the twelfth-century Great West Window, Canterbury Cathedral, Kent, England.

Abraham, depicted here full-length, seated on a wooden stool, is richly-dressed, wearing patterned hose and soft white kid shoes.

Abraham offers Isaac as a sacrifice
Two details from the symbolic thirteenth-century Window of the Redemption, Chartres Cathedral, France.

In the left-hand panel, Isaac is carrying the wood for the altar; in the right-hand panel, the angel is restraining Abraham from sacrificing his son on the altar.

ABRA
ĐO

GENESIS
Chapter 28:10–17

JACOB'S LADDER

AND Jacob went out from Beersheba, and went toward Haran. And he lighted upon a certain place, and tarried there all night, because the sun was set; and he took of the stones of that place, and put them for his pillows, and lay down in that place to sleep. And he dreamed, and behold a ladder set up on the earth, and the top of it reached to heaven: and behold the angels of God ascending and descending on it. And, behold, the LORD stood above it, and said, I am the LORD God of Abraham thy father, and the God of Isaac: the land whereon thou liest, to thee will I give it, and to thy seed; And thy seed shall be as the dust of the earth, and thou shalt spread abroad to the west, and to the east, and to the north, and to the south: and in thee and in thy seed shall all the families of the earth be blessed. And, behold, I am with thee, and will keep thee in all places whither thou goest, and will bring thee again into this land; for I will not leave thee, until I have done that which I have spoken to thee of.

And Jacob awaked out of his sleep, and he said, Surely the LORD is in this place; and I knew it not. And he was afraid, and said, How dreadful is this place! this is none other but the house of God, and this is the gate of heaven.

Jacob's ladder
Swiss roundel, now in Wragby Church, Yorkshire, England; 1685.

This roundel measures only about 20 centimetres (7 inches) in diameter. Jacob, lying asleep, is accompanied by a sleeping hound; in the background is an anachronistic Swiss lakeside town, with landing staithes and a church. Wragby Church today contains the world's largest collection of Swiss stained glass – 489 panels – acquired by a Mr Winn of Nostell Priory after the French invasion of Switzerland in the late eighteenth century.

Joseph in the pit
Seventeenth-century Flemish roundel, Begbroke Church, Oxfordshire, England.

The artist has managed with great ingenuity to include twenty-seven figures in this small roundel, with five of them forcing Joseph into the well-like pit. While those at the centre are violently engaged, some of Joseph's brothers, on the fringes of the crowd, seem to be feigning unconcern.

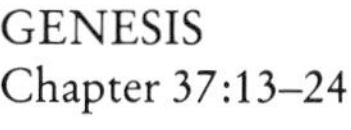

GENESIS
Chapter 37:13–24

JOSEPH AND HIS BROTHERS

AND Israel said unto Joseph, Do not thy brethren feed the flock in Shechem? come, and I will send thee unto them. And he said to him, Here am I. And he said to him, Go, I pray thee, see whether it be well with thy brethren, and well with the flocks; and bring me word again. So he sent him out of the vale of Hebron, and he came to Shechem.

And a certain man found him, and, behold, he was wandering in the field: and the man asked him, saying, What seekest thou? And he said, I seek my brethren: tell me, I pray thee, where they feed their flocks. And the man said, They are departed hence; for I heard them say, Let us go to Dothan. And Joseph went after his brethren, and found them in Dothan. And when they saw him afar off, even before he came near unto them, they conspired against him to slay him. And they said one to another, Behold, this dreamer cometh. Come now therefore, and let us slay him, and cast him into some pit, and we will say, Some evil beast hath devoured him: and we shall see what will become of his dreams. And Reuben heard it, and he delivered him out of their hands; and said, Let us not kill him. And Reuben said unto them, Shed no blood, but cast him into this pit that is in the wilderness, and lay no hand upon him; that he might rid him out of their hands, to deliver him to his father again.

And it came to pass, when Joseph was come unto his brethren, that they stript Joseph out of his coat, his coat of many colours that was on him; And they took him, and cast him into a pit: and the pit was empty, there was no water in it.

GENESIS
Chapter 40:1–23

The butler is brought before Pharaoh
Seventeenth-century Flemish panel, Wells Cathedral, Somerset, England.

The artist has paid much attention to detail; Pharaoh, on a gold throne, is given a sceptre and crown or circlet worn over a domed headpiece; the butler kneels before him. The lips of some of the men are stained red with enamelling.

PHARAOH'S BUTLER'S DREAM

AND it came to pass after these things, that the butler of the king of Egypt and his baker had offended their lord the king of Egypt. And Pharaoh was wroth against two of his officers, against the chief of the butlers, and against the chief of the bakers. And he put them in ward in the house of the captain of the guard, into the prison, the place where Joseph was bound. And the captain of the guard charged Joseph with them, and he served them: and they continued a season in ward.

And they dreamed a dream both of them, each man his dream in one night, each man according to the interpretation of his dream, the butler and the baker of the king of Egypt, which were bound in the prison. And Joseph came in unto them in the morning, and looked upon them, and, behold, they were sad. And he asked Pharaoh's officers that were with him in the ward of his lord's house, saying, Wherefore look ye so sadly to day? And they said unto him, We have dreamed a dream, and there is no interpreter of it. And Joseph said unto them, Do not interpretations belong to God? tell me them, I pray you. And the chief butler told his dream to Joseph, and said to him, In my dream, behold, a vine was before me; And in the vine were three branches: and it was as though it budded, and her blossoms shot forth; and the clusters thereof brought forth ripe grapes: And Pharaoh's cup was in my hand: and I took the grapes, and pressed them into Pharaoh's cup, and I gave the cup into Pharaoh's hand. And Joseph said unto him, This is the interpretation of it: The three branches are three days: Yet within three days shall Pharaoh lift up thine head, and restore thee unto thy place: and thou shalt deliver Pharaoh's cup into his hand, after the former manner when thou wast his butler. But think on me when it shall be well with thee, and shew kindness, I pray thee, unto me, and make mention of me unto Pharaoh, and bring me out of this house: For indeed I was stolen away out of the land of the Hebrews: and here also have I done nothing that they should put me into the dungeon. When the chief baker saw that the interpretation was good, he said unto Joseph, I also was in my dream, and, behold, I had three white baskets on my head: And in the uppermost basket there was of all manner of bakemeats for Pharaoh; and the birds did eat them out of the basket upon my head. And Joseph answered and said, This is the interpretation thereof: The three baskets are three days: Yet within three days shall Pharaoh lift up thy head from off thee, and shall hang thee on a tree; and the birds shall eat thy flesh from off thee.

And it came to pass the third day, which was Pharaoh's birthday, that he made a feast unto all his servants: and he lifted up the head of the chief butler and of the chief baker among his servants. And he restored the chief butler unto his butlership again; and he gave the cup into Pharaoh's hand: But he hanged the chief baker: as Joseph had interpreted to them. Yet did not the chief butler remember Joseph, but forgat him.

MOSES

Now Moses kept the flock of Jethro his father in law, the priest of Midian: and he led the flock to the backside of the desert, and came to the mountain of God, even to Horeb. And the angel of the LORD appeared unto him in a flame of fire out of the midst of a bush: and he looked, and, behold, the bush burned with fire, and the bush was not consumed. And Moses said, I will now turn aside, and see this great sight, why the bush is not burnt. And when the LORD saw that he turned aside to see, God called unto him out of the midst of the bush, and said, Moses, Moses. And he said, Here am I. And he said, Draw not nigh hither: put off thy shoes from off thy feet, for the place whereon thou standest is holy ground. Moreover he said, I am the God of thy father, the God of Abraham, the God of Isaac, and the God of Jacob. And Moses hid his face; for he was afraid to look upon God.

EXODUS
Chapter 3:1–6

Moses and the burning bush
Twelfth-century panel by Master Gerlachus, from the Abbey Church of Arnstein on the Lahn; now in Münster Landesmuseum, Westphalia, Germany.

Moses (*left*) has removed his boots, believing himself on holy ground; his crook has a serpent's head. God speaks from a clump of trees, his head surrounded by a cruciform halo. The window displays great attention to detail and a minute style of execution. Master Gerlachus, the artist, has portrayed himself, paint-brush raised, in rapt concentration; this is the only known signature by a medieval stained-glass artist. The punning inscription calls on God to give light to the artist.

The finding of Moses in the bulrushes
Fifteenth century, Great Malvern Priory, Worcestershire, England.

Pharaoh's daughter is depicted in fifteenth-century royal robes, the baby Moses in swaddling bands. The reed basket is woven in the same way as medieval fences and wattle walls.

FVIR
REXREGV CLARECERE ACHOPROP CIARE
RATVR

EXODUS
Chapter 14:21–27

CROSSING THE RED SEA

AND Moses stretched out his hand over the sea; and the LORD caused the sea to go back by a strong east wind all that night, and made the sea dry land, and the waters were divided. And the children of Israel went into the midst of the sea upon the dry ground: and the waters were a wall unto them on their right hand, and on their left.

And the Egyptians pursued, and went in after them to the midst of the sea, even all Pharaoh's horses, his chariots, and his horsemen. And it came to pass, that in the morning watch the LORD looked unto the host of the Egyptians through the pillar of fire and of the cloud, and troubled the host of the Egyptians, And took off their chariot wheels, that they drave them heavily: so that the Egyptians said, Let us flee from the face of Israel; for the LORD fighteth for them against the Egyptians.

And the LORD said unto Moses, Stretch out thine hand over the sea, that the waters may come again upon the Egyptians, upon their chariots, and upon their horsemen. And Moses stretched forth his hand over the sea, and the sea returned to his strength when the morning appeared; and the Egyptians fled against it; and the LORD overthrew the Egyptians in the midst of the sea.

Manna from Heaven
Fifteenth-century window in Great Malvern Priory, Worcestershire, England.

In this strange scene, manna falls in large egg-sized balls from the sky into the outstretched arms of men below; other figures have already gathered their manna in wooden goblets. This panel has been clumsily patched with gold-coloured glass, which is inappropriately decorated with boots from some other picture!

Moses crosses the Red Sea
Detail from the thirteenth-century East Window of the North Choir Aisle, Lincoln Cathedral, Lincolnshire, England.

In this small roundel, a few figures serve to represent the crowds present at this dramatic episode. Moses is depicted, as frequently elsewhere, with horns adorning his head. Notice the child carried on a man's shoulders. White glass is used to denote those drowned in the engulfing waters; a dog, with staring eyes, denotes terror.

THE TEN COMMANDMENTS

AND God spake all these words, saying, I am the LORD thy God, which have brought thee out of the land of Egypt, out of the house of bondage. Thou shalt have no other gods before me. Thou shalt not make unto thee any graven image, or any likeness of any thing that is in heaven above, or that is in the earth beneath, or that is in the water under the earth: Thou shalt not bow down thyself to them, nor serve them: for I the LORD thy God am a jealous God, visiting the iniquity of the fathers upon the children unto the third and fourth generation of them that hate me; And shewing

EXODUS
Chapter 20:1–17

Moses on Mount Sinai
Twentieth-century window by Hans Gottfried von Stockhausen in the Besserer Chapel, Ulm Cathedral, West Germany.

Moses, atop Mount Sinai, cups his ears to hear God's voice; the people are separated from God by a thick band of purple cloud. The tiny Besserer Chapel was built by Ulrich von Ensingen for the Ulm merchant Eitel Besserer. Jacob Acker worked on several windows for the Besserer Chapel around 1430; his son, Hans, continued in his father's craft, also creating a series of windows for Ulm Minster choir. Von Stockhausen, who lives at Esslingen, near Stuttgart, has added a number of panels.

The Golden Calf
Detail from an eighteenth-century window painted by Joshua Price, in Great Witley Church, Worcestershire, England.

A spurious Classicism marks the working style of painted glass by Joshua Price. This window shows the idolatrous Israelites worshipping the Golden Calf.

mercy unto thousands of them that love me, and keep my commandments. Thou shalt not take the name of the LORD thy God in vain; for the LORD will not hold him guiltless that taketh his name in vain. Remember the sabbath day, to keep it holy. Six days shalt thou labour, and do all thy work: But the seventh day is the sabbath of the LORD thy God: in it thou shalt not do any work, thou, nor thy son, nor thy daughter, thy manservant, nor thy maidservant, nor thy cattle, nor thy stranger that is within thy gates: For in six days the LORD made heaven and earth, the sea, and all that in them is, and rested the seventh day: wherefore the LORD blessed the sabbath day, and hallowed it.

Honour thy father and thy mother: that thy days may be long upon the land which the LORD thy God giveth thee. Thou shalt not kill. Thou shalt not commit adultery. Thou shalt not steal. Thou shalt not bear false witness against thy neighbour. Thou shalt not covet thy neighbour's house, thou shalt not covet thy neighbour's wife, nor his manservant, nor his maidservant, nor his ox, nor his ass, nor any thing that is thy neighbour's.

SPYING OUT THE LAND

NUMBERS
Chapter 13:17–30

AND Moses sent them to spy out the land of Canaan, and said unto them, Get you up this way southward, and go up into the mountain: And see the land, what it is; and the people that dwelleth therein, whether they be strong or weak, few or many; And what the land is that they dwell in, whether it be good or bad; and what cities they be that they dwell in, whether in tents, or in strong holds; And what the land is, whether it be fat or lean, whether there be wood therein, or not. And be ye of good courage, and bring of the fruit of the land. Now the time was the time of the firstripe grapes.

So they went up, and searched the land from the wilderness of Zin unto Rehob, as men come to Hamath. And they ascended by the south, and came unto Hebron; where Ahiman, Sheshai, and Talmai, the children of Anak, were. (Now Hebron was built seven years before Zoan in Egypt.) And they came unto the brook of Eshcol, and cut down from thence a

The two spies return from the Promised Land
Sixteenth-century window from Marston Bigot Church, Somerset, England.

One of the finest stained-glass representations of this story, the human figures are all meticulously observed. The journeyings and adventures of the spies are witnessed to by their torn hose and worn shoes. The pruning hook in one spy's belt was presumably used to cut the vast bunch of grapes, which represent the fertility of the vineyards of Canaan. Some of the waiting Israelites look decidedly sceptical. Moses' classic 'horns' (*see above*) are here represented by upcurling strands of his thick hair.

Moses and Joshua
Panel from the Rieter Window, Church of St Lawrence, Nuremberg, Germany; 1479.

Moses, richly dressed in fine cloth, leads his successor, the fully-armoured Joshua, by the hand; Joshua hangs back with becoming modesty. The apparent 'mushrooms' (*top left*) are medieval Jewish headgear. In this window the figures stand out strikingly from their background; the white architectural elements are less prominent than elsewhere. This window was presented to the Church of St Lawrence by the Rieter family.

branch with one cluster of grapes, and they bare it between two upon a staff; and they brought of the pomegranates, and of the figs. The place was called the brook Eshcol, because of the cluster of grapes which the children of Israel cut down from thence. And they returned from searching of the land after forty days.

And they went and came to Moses, and to Aaron, and to all the congregation of the children of Israel, unto the wilderness of Paran, to Kadesh; and brought back word unto them, and unto all the congregation, and shewed them the fruit of the land. And they told him, and said, We came unto the land whither thou sentest us, and surely it floweth with milk and honey; and this is the fruit of it. Nevertheless the people be strong that dwell in the land, and the cities are walled, and very great: and moreover we saw the children of Anak there. The Amalekites dwell in the land of the south: and the Hittites, and the Jebusites, and the Amorites, dwell in the mountains: and the Canaanites dwell by the sea, and by the coast of Jordan. And Caleb stilled the people before Moses, and said, Let us go up at once, and possess it; for we are well able to overcome it.

JERICHO IS TAKEN

JOSHUA
Chapter 6:1–7

Now Jericho was straitly shut up because of the children of Israel: none went out, and none came in. And the LORD said unto Joshua, See, I have given into thine hand Jericho, and the king thereof, and the mighty men of valour. And ye shall compass the city, all ye men of war, and go round about the city once. Thus shalt thou do six days. And seven priests shall bear before the ark seven trumpets of rams' horns: and the seventh day ye shall compass the city seven times, and the priests shall blow with the trumpets. And it shall come to pass, that when they make a long blast with the ram's horn, and when ye hear the sound of the trumpet, all the people shall shout with a great shout; and the wall of the city shall fall down flat, and the people shall ascend up every man straight before him.

And Joshua the son of Nun called the priests, and said unto them, Take up the ark of the covenant, and let seven priests bear seven trumpets of rams' horns before the ark of the LORD. And he said unto the people, Pass on, and compass the city, and let him that is armed pass on before the ark of the LORD.

Balaam meets an angel on the road
Flemish panel from Herckenrode; now in St Mary's Church, Shrewsbury, Shropshire, England; 1551.

Balaam is depicted wearing a jewelled coronet, and about to strike his donkey angrily with a short sceptre. The donkey's jaw is open to show it is protesting at being driven towards the angel, who brandishes an ornate sword. The town is shown as a medieval fortified city, complete with arrow-slits and tiny dormer windows.

The walls of Jericho
Nineteenth-century window in Lincoln Cathedral, England.

The Israelites are blowing their rams' horns outside the city, before the city fell. In the background of the right-hand panel is the burning city of Ai (Joshua 18:19–21). The scene in the foreground shows either the building of the altar (Joshua 8:30–31) or the covenant with the men of Gibeon (Joshua 9).

SAMSON

AND Samson went down to Timnath, and saw a woman in Timnath of the daughters of the Philistines. And he came up, and told his father and his mother, and said, I have seen a woman in Timnath of the daughters of the Philistines: now therefore get her for me to wife. Then his father and his mother said unto him, Is there never a woman among the daughters of thy brethren, or among all my people, that thou goest to take a wife of the uncircumcised Philistines? And Samson said unto his father, Get her for me; for she pleaseth me well. But his father and his mother knew not that it was of the LORD, that he sought an occasion against the Philistines: for at that time the Philistines had dominion over Israel.

Then went Samson down, and his father and his mother, to Timnath, and came to the vineyards of Timnath: and, behold, a young lion roared against him.

And the Spirit of the LORD came mightily upon him, and he rent him as he would have rent a kid, and he had nothing in his hand: but he told not his father or his mother what he had done.

JUDGES
Chapter 14:1–6

Gideon and the fleece
Detail from a fourteenth-century window in the Frauenkirche, Esslingen, Swabia, Germany.

A simple, clearly-drawn composition. Gideon is dressed in tunic, cloak, hose and boots, and holds the fully-skinned sheep's fleece and pelt.

Samson and the lion
Fourteeenth-century German panel in the Church of St Etienne, Mulhouse, Alsace, France.

The amply-muscled Samson, sporting a forester's long-brimmed scarlet hat on his luxuriant head of hair, wrestles with a distinctly heraldic-looking lion.

Samson and the gates of Gaza
Detail from the thirteenth-century Redemption Window, North Aisle, Chartres Cathedral, France.

In this window, Samson is depicted as astonishingly slim for so strong a man. This was a favourite motif in the Middle Ages; people believed it alluded to the opening of the doors of graves by the risen Christ.

JUDGES
Chapter 16:1–3

SAMSON AT GAZA

THEN went Samson to Gaza, and saw there an harlot, and went in unto her. And it was told the Gazites, saying, Samson is come hither. And they compassed him in, and laid wait for him all night in the gate of the city, and were quiet all the night, saying, In the morning, when it is day, we shall kill him. And Samson lay till midnight, and arose at midnight, and took the doors of the gate of the city, and the two posts, and went away with them, bar and all, and put them upon his shoulders, and carried them up to the top of an hill that is before Hebron.

SAMUEL

AND the child Samuel ministered unto the LORD before Eli. And the word of the LORD was precious in those days; there was no open vision. And it came to pass at that time, when Eli was laid down in his place, and his eyes began to wax dim, that he could not see; And ere the lamp of God went out in the temple of the LORD, where the ark of God was, and Samuel was laid down to sleep; That the LORD called Samuel: and he answered, Here am I. And he ran unto Eli, and said, Here am I; for thou calledst me. And he said, I called not; lie down again. And he went and lay down. And the LORD called yet again, Samuel. And Samuel arose and went to Eli, and said, Here am I; for thou didst call me. And he answered, I called not, my son; lie down again. Now Samuel did not yet know the LORD, neither was the word of the LORD yet revealed unto him. And the LORD called Samuel again the third time. And he arose and went to Eli, and said, Here am I; for thou didst call me. And Eli perceived that the LORD had called the child. Therefore Eli said unto Samuel, Go, lie down: and it shall be, if he call thee, that thou shalt say, Speak, LORD; for thy servant heareth. So Samuel went and lay down in his place. And the LORD came, and stood, and called as at other times, Samuel, Samuel. Then Samuel answered, Speak; for thy servant heareth.

And the LORD said to Samuel, Behold, I will do a thing in Israel, at which both the ears of every one that heareth it shall tingle. In that day I will perform against Eli all things which I have spoken concerning his house: when I begin, I will also make an end. For I have told him that I will judge his house for ever for the iniquity which he knoweth; because his sons made themselves vile, and he restrained them not. And therefore I have sworn unto the house of Eli, that the iniquity of Eli's house shall not be purged with sacrifice nor offering for ever.

And Samuel lay until the morning, and opened the doors of the house of the LORD. And Samuel feared to shew Eli the vision. Then Eli called Samuel, and said, Samuel, my son. And he answered, Here am I. And he said, What is the thing that the LORD hath said unto thee? I pray thee hide it not from me: God do so to thee, and more also, if thou hide any thing from me of all the things that he said unto thee. And Samuel told him every whit, and hid nothing from him. And he said, It is the LORD: let him do what seemeth him good.

And Samuel grew, and the LORD was with him, and did let none of his words fall to the ground. And all Israel from Dan even to Beersheba knew that Samuel was established to be a prophet of the LORD. And the LORD appeared again in Shiloh: for the LORD revealed himself to Samuel in Shiloh by the word of the LORD.

1 SAMUEL
Chapter 3:1–21

The boy Samuel is presented to Eli
A roundel from the thirteenth-century 'Poor Man's Bible Window' No.1, North Choir Aisle, Canterbury Cathedral, Kent, England.

A roundel presents a particular artistic challenge: to portray concisely and clearly a classic scene within a limited space. Here, Samuel's family have brought the boy to serve in the Temple, and have also brought as gifts three rams. Other offerings include urns of grain.

Eli and the boy Samuel
Nineteenth-century window in Lincoln Cathedral, England.

The sleeping Eli does not hear God's voice; the child kneels to listen to God's message to him. The 'Veil of the Temple', guarding the Holy of Holies, seems to be drawn aside, to symbolize this moment of God's self-revelation to Samuel. The seven-branched candlestick, or menorah, also symbolizes God's presence.

HERODIS REGINA SABEI
+SIGNIFICAT DOM
TRINVM
BLATIO

1 SAMUEL
Chapter 19:8–10

KING SAUL

AND there was war again: and David went out, and fought with the Philistines, and slew them with a great slaughter; and they fled from him. And the evil spirit from the LORD was upon Saul, as he sat in his house with his javelin in his hand: and David played with his hand. And Saul sought to smite David even to the wall with the javelin; but he slipped away out of Saul's presence, and he smote the javelin into the wall: and David fled, and escaped that night.

Saul attempts to spear David
Fourteenth-century German panel in the Church of St Etienne, Mulhouse, Alsace, France.

King Saul is portrayed almost cross-eyed with anger, about to hurl his spear at the young harpist, who seems ready to flee on an instant. The distance between the two figures has been graphically foreshortened.

1 SAMUEL
Chapter 31:1–7

THE DEATH OF SAUL

Now the Philistines fought against Israel: and the men of Israel fled from before the Philistines, and fell down slain in mount Gilboa. And the Philistines followed hard upon Saul and upon his sons; and the Philistines slew Jonathan, and Abinadab, and Malchishua, Saul's sons. And the battle went sore against Saul, and the archers hit him; and he was sore wounded of the archers. Then said Saul unto his armourbearer, Draw thy sword, and thrust me through therewith; lest these uncircumcised come and thrust me through, and abuse me. But his armourbearer would not; for he was sore afraid. Therefore Saul took a sword, and fell upon it. And when his armourbearer saw that Saul was dead, he fell likewise upon his sword, and died with him. So Saul died, and his three sons, and his armourbearer, and all his men, that same day together.

And when the men of Israel that were on the other side of the valley, and they that were on the other side Jordan, saw that the men of Israel fled, and that Saul and his sons were dead, they forsook the cities, and fled; and the Philistines came and dwelt in them.

King Saul
Detail from a thirteenth-century lancet below the North Rose Window, Chartres Cathedral, France.

Saul's kingship is symbolized by his red, royal blue and gold robes. The design focuses on the white blade of the great two-handed sword with which Saul is killing himself, after the defeat of Israel's army by the Philistines on Mount Gilboa. The king's left hand is raised in a final farewell gesture.

THE ANCESTORS OF JESUS

THE book of the generation of Jesus Christ, the son of David, the son of Abraham. Abraham begat Isaac; and Isaac begat Jacob; and Jacob begat Judas and his brethren; And Judas begat Phares and Zara of Thamar; and Phares begat Esrom; and Esrom begat Aram; And Aram begat Aminadab; and Aminadab begat Naasson; and Naasson begat Salmon; And Salmon begat Booz of Rachab; and Booz begat Obed of Ruth; and Obed begat Jesse; And Jesse begat David the king; and David the king begat Solomon of her that had been the wife of Urias; And Solomon begat Roboam; and Roboam begat Abia; and Abia begat Asa; And Asa begat Josaphat; and Josaphat begat Joram; and Joram begat Ozias; And Ozias begat Joatham; and Joatham begat Achaz; and Achaz begat Ezekias; And Ezekias begat Manasses; and Manasses begat Amon; and Amon begat Josias; And Josias begat Jechonias and his brethren, about the time they were carried away to Babylon: And after they were brought to Babylon, Jechonias begat Salathiel; and Salathiel begat Zorobabel; And Zorobabel begat Abiud; and Abiud begat Eliakim; and Eliakim begat Azor; And Azor begat Sadoc; and Sadoc begat Achim; and Achim begat Eliud; And Eliud begat Eleazar; and Eleazar begat Matthan; and Matthan begat Jacob; And Jacob begat Joseph the husband of Mary, of whom was born Jesus, who is called Christ. So all the generations from Abraham to David are fourteen generations; and from David until the carrying away into Babylon are fourteen generations; and from the carrying away into Babylon unto Christ are fourteen generations.

Now the birth of Jesus Christ was on this wise: When as his mother Mary was espoused to Joseph, before they came together, she was found with child of the Holy Ghost. Then Joseph her husband, being a just man, and not willing to make her a publick example, was minded to put her away privily. But while he thought on these things, behold, the angel of the Lord appeared unto him in a dream, saying, Joseph, thou son of David, fear not to take unto thee Mary thy wife: for that which is conceived in her is of the Holy Ghost. And she shall bring forth a son, and thou shalt call his name JESUS: for he shall save his people from their sins. Now all this was done, that it might be fulfilled which was spoken of the Lord by the prophet, saying, Behold, a virgin shall be with child, and shall bring forth a son, and they shall call his name Emmanuel, which being interpreted is, God with us. Then Joseph being raised from sleep did as the angel of the Lord had bidden him, and took unto him his wife: And knew her not till she had brought forth her firstborn son: and he called his name JESUS.

MATTHEW
Chapter 1:1–25

The Tree of Jesse
Lancet Window, West End of Nave, Chartres Cathedral, Ile de France, France; 1140–50, restored.

Probably the best example anywhere of this subject, Christ's roots are traced back to Jesse, at the bottom of the window. The stem of his family tree grows from Jesse's groin; above him are panels representing four kings of Judah, Mary, and at the top, Jesus, surrounded by seven white doves, symbolizing the gifts of the Spirit. Fourteen prophets, who foretold the coming of the Messiah, flank the tree, in glass half-medallions.

DAVID

AND it came to pass, when the Philistine arose, and came and drew nigh to meet David, that David hasted, and ran toward the army to meet the Philistine. And David put his hand in his bag, and took thence a stone, and slang it, and smote the Philistine in his forehead, that the stone sunk into his forehead; and he fell upon his face to the earth. So David prevailed over the Philistine with a sling and with a stone, and smote the Philistine, and slew him; but there was no sword in the hand of David. Therefore David ran, and stood upon the Philistine, and took his sword, and drew it out of the sheath thereof, and slew him, and cut off his head therewith. And when the Philistines saw their champion was dead, they fled.

1 SAMUEL
Chapter 17:48–51

David and Goliath
Twentieth-century window in the Church of St Peter Mancroft, Norwich, Norfolk, England.

Although portrayed in a highly stylized manner, the human figures in this window are pictured with a keenly-observed attention to detail. David is simply equipped with a shepherd's crook, water-bottle and leather sling; Goliath, already collapsing from his head-wound, in contrast boasts a vast shield featuring a grimacing pagan deity, a two-handed broadsword, massive spear and heavy metal greaves.

David and Goliath
Panel from Edward Burne-Jones' Vyner Memorial Window, in the Lady Chapel, Christ Church Cathedral, Oxford, England; 1872–3.

The Vyner window, with full-length portraits of Samuel, David, John and Timothy, and smaller scenes below, of each man in his youth, commemorates a nineteenth-century Oxford undergraduate murdered by bandits in Greece. In the window Burne-Jones has succeeded in making the lead-lines a vital part of the design. In this panel, the artist contrasts powerfully the barbaric giant with the youthful hero, his face set and purposeful.

DAVID

David escapes from Saul
Detail from the thirteenth-century Bible Window, Chapel of Saints and Martyrs of Our Own Time, Canterbury Cathedral, Kent, England.

Michal helps David to flee
Fourteenth-century German panel from the Church of St Etienne, Mulhouse, Alsace, France.

David is portrayed as surprisingly small. Michal is preventing two soldiers, fully-armoured in medieval style and brandishing halberds (axes), from entering in pursuit of David.

1 SAMUEL
Chapter 19:11–16

SAUL also sent messengers unto David's house, to watch him, and to slay him in the morning: and Michal David's wife told him, saying, If thou save not thy life to night, to morrow thou shalt be slain.

So Michal let David down through a window: and he went, and fled, and escaped. And Michal took an image, and laid it in the bed, and put a pillow of goats' hair for his bolster, and covered it with a cloth. And when Saul sent messengers to take David, she said, He is sick. And Saul sent the messengers again to see David, saying, Bring him up to me in the bed, that I may slay him. And when the messengers were come in, behold, there was an image in the bed, with a pillow of goats' hair for his bolster.

1 SAMUEL
Chapter 22:1–7

DAVID therefore departed thence, and escaped to the cave Adullam: and when his brethren and all his father's house heard it, they went down thither to him. And every one that was in distress, and every one that was in debt, and every one that was discontented, gathered themselves unto him; and he became a captain over them: and there were with him about four hundred men. And David went thence to Mizpeh of Moab: and he said unto the king of Moab, Let my father and my mother, I pray thee, come forth, and be with you, till I know what God will do for me. And he brought them before the king of Moab: and they dwelt with him all the while that David was in the hold.

And the prophet Gad said unto David, Abide not in the hold; depart, and get thee into the land of Judah. Then David departed, and came into the forest of Hareth.

King David
Detail from the Solomon Panel, now in the Münster Landesmuseum, Germany; 1360–70.

David is caught here apparently scowling; he is dressed in a short white shoulder cape, which does not have the characteristic fleck-marks to indicate royal ermine.

King David
Detail from the Jesse Tree Window, St Dyfnog's Church, Llanrhaeadr, North Wales; 1533.

King David is here portrayed as a melancholy harpist, and eccentrically dressed, wearing a coronet over a woven cap, an ermine-trimmed cloak and lime green hose.

SOLOMON

1 KINGS Chapter 10:1–13

AND when the queen of Sheba heard of the fame of Solomon concerning the name of the LORD, she came to prove him with hard questions. And she came to Jerusalem with a very great train, with camels that bare spices, and very much gold, and precious stones: and when she was come to Solomon, she communed with him of all that was in her heart. And Solomon told her all her questions: there was not any thing hid from the king, which he told her not. And when the queen of Sheba had seen all Solomon's wisdom, and the house that he had built, And the meat of his table, and the sitting of his servants, and the attendance of his ministers, and their apparel, and his cupbearers, and his ascent by which he went up unto the house of the LORD; there was no more spirit in her. And she said to the king, It was a true report that I heard in mine own land of thy acts and of thy wisdom. Howbeit I believed not the words, until I came, and mine eyes had seen it: and, behold, the half was not told me: thy wisdom and prosperity exceedeth the fame which I heard. Happy are thy men, happy are these thy servants, which stand continually before thee, and that hear thy wisdom. Blessed be the LORD thy God which delighted in thee, to set thee on the throne of Israel: because the LORD loved Israel for ever, therefore made he thee king, to do judgment and justice. And she gave the king an hundred and twenty talents of gold, and of spices very great store, and precious stones: there came no more such abundance of spices as these which the queen of Sheba gave to king Solomon. And the navy also of Hiram, that brought gold from Ophir, brought in from Ophir great plenty of almug trees, and precious stones. And the king made of the almug trees pillars for the house of the LORD, and for the king's house, harps also and psalteries for singers: there came no such almug trees, nor were seen unto this day. And king Solomon gave unto the queen of Sheba all her desire, whatsoever she asked, beside that which Solomon gave her of his royal bounty. So she turned and went to her own country, she and her servants.

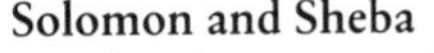

Solomon and Sheba
Window by Wouter Crabeth, from St John's Church, Gouda, The Netherlands; 1561.

Solomon's throne is set with royal lions of Judah and heavily guarded by soldiers. Camels from the Queen of Sheba's caravan may be seen in the background, through an embrasure. This was the first window to be completed by Wouter, younger of the celebrated Crabeth brothers, who were jointly responsible for fourteen of the major windows in this church.

REHOBOAM AND JEROBOAM

AND king Rehoboam consulted with the old men, that stood before Solomon his father while he yet lived, and said, How do ye advise that I may answer this people? And they spake unto him, saying, If thou wilt be a servant unto this people this day, and wilt serve them, and answer them, and speak good words to them, then they will be thy servants for ever. But he forsook the counsel of the old men, which they had given him, and consulted with the young men that were grown up with him, and which stood before him: And he said unto them, What counsel give ye that we may answer this people, who have spoken to me, saying, Make the yoke which thy father did put upon us lighter? And the young men that were grown up with him spake unto him, saying, Thus shalt thou speak unto this people that spake unto thee, saying, Thy father made our yoke heavy, but make thou it lighter unto us; thus shalt thou say unto them, My little finger shall be thicker than my father's loins. And now whereas my father did lade you with a heavy yoke, I will add to your yoke: my father hath chastised you with whips, but I will chastise you with scorpions.

1 KINGS
Chapter 12:6–11

King Rehoboam
Detail from the Great West Window, Canterbury Cathedral, Kent, England; c.1190.

Rehoboam is seated, but has no crown; his soft, green leather ankle boots are typical of this date.

King Jeroboam is warned by a prophet
Panel from the thirteenth-century Poor Man's Bible Window, Canterbury Cathedral, Kent, England.

King Jeroboam has already cut the throat of the sacrificial lamb. The young prophet carries a scroll, perhaps symbolizing his message of warning to the king (1 Kings 12:25–13:32).

RO OAS

ELIJAH AND ELISHA

2 KINGS
Chapter 2:1–15

AND it came to pass, when the LORD would take up Elijah into heaven by a whirlwind, that Elijah went with Elisha from Gilgal. And Elijah said unto Elisha, Tarry here, I pray thee; for the LORD hath sent me to Bethel. And Elisha said unto him, As the LORD liveth, and as thy soul liveth, I will not leave thee. So they went down to Bethel. And the sons of the prophets that were at Bethel came forth to Elisha, and said unto him, Knowest thou that the LORD will take away thy master from thy head to day? And he said, Yea, I know it; hold ye your peace. And Elijah said unto him, Elisha, tarry here, I pray thee; for the LORD hath sent me to Jericho. And he said, As the LORD liveth, and as thy soul liveth, I will not leave thee. So they came to Jericho. And the sons of the prophets that were at Jericho came to Elisha, and said unto him, Knowest thou that the LORD will take away thy master from thy head to day? And he answered, Yea, I know it; hold ye your peace. And Elijah said unto him, Tarry, I pray thee, here; for the LORD hath sent me to Jordan. And he said, As the LORD liveth, and as thy soul liveth, I will not leave thee. And they two went on. And fifty men of the sons of the prophets went, and stood to view afar off: and they two stood by Jordan. And Elijah took his mantle, and wrapped it together, and smote the waters, and they were divided hither and thither, so that they two went over on dry ground.

And it came to pass, when they were gone over, that Elijah said unto Elisha, Ask what I shall do for thee, before I be taken away from thee. And Elisha said, I pray thee, let a double portion of thy spirit be upon me. And he said, Thou hast asked a hard thing: nevertheless, if thou see me when I am taken from thee, it shall be so unto thee; but if not, it shall not be so. And it came to pass, as they still went on, and talked, that, behold, there appeared a chariot of fire, and horses of fire, and parted them both asunder; and Elijah went up by a whirlwind into heaven.

Elijah is taken up in a chariot of fire
Panel now in the Münster Landesmuseum, Germany; 1360–70.

Elijah's 'chariot' – surrounded by flames but not consumed – is an accurate representation of a fourteenth-century cart, with its four wooden wheels and its steering yoke operated by the driver's feet. The bald Elijah's long white mantle – the symbol of his authority – is just falling to his successor Elisha, below.

Elijah and Elisha
Detail from a seventeenth-century window by Abraham Van Linge, University College Chapel, Oxford, England.

It is all too clear that this window was made of 'painted glass' since the paint in places is visibly peeling away. The prophet Elijah passes his cloak to the barefooted Elisha, depicted in three different positions below. From their unconcern, we can only think that the artist intended us to believe that the other people could not see the fiery chariot.

And Elisha saw it, and he cried, My father, my father, the chariot of Israel, and the horsemen thereof. And he saw him no more: and he took hold of his own clothes, and rent them in two pieces. He took up also the mantle of Elijah that fell from him, and went back, and stood by the bank of Jordan; And he took the mantle of Elijah that fell from him, and smote the waters, and said, Where is the LORD God of Elijah? and when he also had smitten the waters, they parted hither and thither: and Elisha went over. And when the sons of the prophets which were to view at Jericho saw him, they said, The spirit of Elijah doth rest on Elisha. And they came to meet him, and bowed themselves to the ground before him.

The prophet Isaiah
Panel from the fourteenth-century East Window, Exeter Cathedral, Devon, England.

Isaiah points to a scroll, which refers to the Stump of Jesse (Isaiah 11:1).

DANIEL

THEN the king commanded, and they brought Daniel, and cast him into the den of lions. Now the king spake and said unto Daniel, Thy God whom thou servest continually, he will deliver thee. And a stone was brought, and laid upon the mouth of the den; and the king sealed it with his own signet, and with the signet of his lords; that the purpose might not be changed concerning Daniel.

Then the king went to his palace, and passed the night fasting: neither were instruments of musick brought before him: and his sleep went from him. Then the king arose very early in the morning, and went in haste unto the den of lions. And when he came to the den, he cried with a lamentable voice unto Daniel: and the king spake and said to Daniel, O Daniel, servant of the living God, is thy God, whom thou servest continually, able to deliver thee from the lions? Then said Daniel unto the king, O king, live for ever. My God hath sent his angel, and hath shut the lions' mouths, that they have not hurt me: forasmuch as before him innocency was found in me; and also before thee, O king, have I done no hurt. Then was the king exceeding glad for him, and commanded that they should take Daniel up out of the den. So Daniel was taken up out of the den, and no manner of hurt was found upon him, because he believed in his God.

DANIEL
Chapter 6:16–23

Daniel in the lion's den
Fourteenth-century German panel from the Church of St Etienne, Mulhouse, Alsace, France.

Daniel is shown receiving food. An apocryphal story had it that an angel brought the prophet Habakkuk (*left*) to Babylon by his hair. The surrounding lions appear decidedly ferocious.

DANIEL
Chapter 3:26–28

The burning, fiery furnace
Seventeenth-century roundel, now in the Darmstadt Museum, Germany.

This roundel is remarkable for its intricate detail; see, for example, Nebuchadnezzar's armour, with the face of a pagan deity embossed on his shoulder, and the soldier's quiverful of arrows. The city is decorated with anachronistic Islamic crescents, to show its Eastern location. The three Hebrew victims are clearly visible, accompanied by the fourth figure, while the flames belching from the furnace drive back the peasant onlookers.

THEN Nebuchadnezzar came near to the mouth of the burning fiery furnace, and spake, and said, Shadrach, Meshach, and Abed-nego, ye servants of the most high God, come forth, and come hither. Then Shadrach, Meshach, and Abed-nego, came forth of the midst of the fire. And the princes, governors, and captains, and the king's counsellers, being gathered together, saw these men, upon whose bodies the fire had no power, nor was an hair of their head singed, neither were their coats changed, nor the smell of fire had passed on them. Then Nebuchadnezzar spake, and said, Blessed be the God of Shadrach, Meshach, and Abed-nego, who hath sent his angel, and delivered his servants that trusted in him, and have changed the king's word, and yielded their bodies, that they might not serve nor worship any god, except their own God.

AMOS

THE words of Amos, who was among the herdmen of Tekoa, which he saw concerning Israel in the days of Uzziah king of Judah, and in the days of Jeroboam the son of Joash king of Israel, two years before the earthquake. And he said, The LORD will roar from Zion, and utter his voice from Jerusalem; and the habitations of the shepherds shall mourn, and the top of Carmel shall wither. Thus saith the LORD; For three transgressions of Damascus, and for four, I will not turn away the punishment thereof; because they have threshed Gilead with threshing instruments of iron: But I will send a fire into the house of Hazael, which shall devour the palaces of Benhadad. I will break also the bar of Damascus, and cut off the inhabitant from the plain of Aven, and him that holdeth the sceptre from the house of Eden: and the people of Syria shall go into captivity unto Kir, saith the LORD.

Thus saith the LORD; For three transgressions of Gaza, and for four, I will not turn away the punishment thereof; because they carried away captive the whole captivity, to deliver them up to Edom: But I will send a fire on the wall of Gaza, which shall devour the palaces thereof: And I will cut off the inhabitant from Ashdod, and him that holdeth the sceptre from Ashkelon, and I will turn mine hand against Ekron: and the remnant of the Philistines shall perish, saith the Lord GOD.

Thus saith the LORD; For three transgressions of Tyrus, and for four, I will not turn away the punishment thereof; because they delivered up the whole captivity to Edom, and remembered not the brotherly covenant: But I will send a fire on the wall of Tyrus, which shall devour the palaces thereof.

Thus saith the LORD; For three transgressions of Edom, and for four, I will not turn away the punishment thereof; because he did pursue his brother with the sword, and did cast off all pity, and his anger did tear perpetually, and he kept his wrath for ever: But I will send a fire upon Teman, which shall devour the palaces of Bozrah.

Thus saith the LORD; For three transgressions of the children of Ammon, and for four, I will not turn away the punishment thereof; because they have ripped up the women with child of Gilead, that they might enlarge their border: But I will kindle a fire in the wall of Rabbah, and it shall devour the palaces thereof, with shouting in the day of battle, with a tempest in the day of the whirlwind: And their king shall go into captivity, he and his princes together, saith the LORD.

AMOS
Chapter 1:1–15

The call of Amos
Panel from Herckenrode, Belgium; now in St Mary's Church, Shrewsbury, Shropshire, England; 1551.

Amos is portrayed dressed in the robes of a wealthy man, in pastures some distance from two fortified chateaux. He kneels, having removed his hat in reverence. Some of the nearby sheep and shepherds are thrown into consternation by the appearance of the heavenly messenger.

JONAH

Now the LORD had prepared a great fish to swallow up Jonah. And Jonah was in the belly of the fish three days and three nights.

Then Jonah prayed unto the LORD his God out of the fish's belly, And said, I cried by reason of mine affliction unto the LORD, and he heard me; out of the belly of hell cried I, and thou heardest my voice. For thou hadst cast me into the deep, in the midst of the seas; and the floods compassed me about: all thy billows and thy waves passed over me. Then I said, I am cast out of thy sight; yet I will look again toward thy holy temple. The waters compassed me about, even to the soul: the depth closed me round about, the weeds were wrapped about my head. I went down to the bottoms of the mountains; the earth with her bars was about me for ever: yet hast thou brought up my life from corruption, O LORD my God. When my soul fainted within me I remembered the LORD: and my prayer came in unto thee, into thine holy temple. They that observe lying vanities forsake their own mercy. But I will sacrifice unto thee with the voice of thanksgiving; I will pay that that I have vowed. Salvation is of the LORD.

And the LORD spake unto the fish, and it vomited out Jonah upon the dry land.

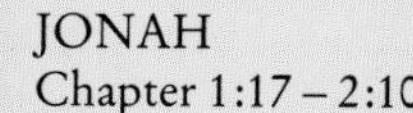

JONAH
Chapter 1:17 – 2:10

Jonah and the great fish
Fourteenth-century German panel from the Church of St Etienne, Mulhouse, Alsace, France.

Jonah is depicted here as an old man, waist-deep in the jaws of the grotesque great fish, his hands in the stylized position of prayer, big eyes gazing skyward in supplication.

Jonah is thrown overboard
Thirteenth-century panel from the centre window of the Corona, Canterbury Cathedral, Kent, England.

The sea is white with breakers, and the ship's sail has been reefed because of the dangerous storm. Jonah again gazes heavenwards as he holds out his hands in supplication for deliverance.

JOHN
Chapter 1:1–14

THE NEW TESTAMENT

In the beginning was the Word, and the Word was with God, and the Word was God. The same was in the beginning with God. All things were made by him; and without him was not any thing made that was made. In him was life; and the life was the light of men. And the light shineth in darkness; and the darkness comprehended it not.

There was a man sent from God, whose name was John. The same came for a witness, to bear witness of the Light, that all men through him might believe. He was not that Light, but was sent to bear witness of that Light. That was the true Light, which lighteth every man that cometh into the world. He was in the world, and the world was made by him, and the world knew him not. He came unto his own, and his own received him not. But as many as received him, to them gave he power to become the sons of God, even to them that believe on his name: Which were born, not of blood, nor of the will of the flesh, nor of the will of man, but of God. And the Word was made flesh, and dwelt among us, (and we beheld his glory, the glory as of the only begotten of the Father,) full of grace and truth.

Christ in majesty
Thirteenth-century panel in the Chapel of the Saints and Martyrs of our Time, Canterbury Cathedral, Kent, England.

Christ is seated on a throne and holds in his left hand the 'Book of the Covenant of the New Testament'. The four Evangelists are represented symbolically (*reading anti-clockwise*) by a winged man (Matthew); a winged lion (Mark); a winged bull (Luke); and an eagle (John). The symbolic figures all look towards Christ, their inspiration.

Matthew and Mark

Matthew
Panel from a sixteenth-century South Aisle Window, parish church of St Neot, Cornwall, England.

Matthew holds his symbol of a human figure.

Mark
Panel from a sixteenth-century South Aisle Window, parish church of St Neot, Cornwall, England.

Mark points to his symbol, the winged lion, familiar to us as the symbol of medieval Venice.

Luke
Panel from a sixteenth-century South Aisle Window, parish church of St Neot, Cornwall, England.

Luke, portrayed here with a calm demeanour, and with his symbol, the ox.

John
Panel from a sixteenth-century South Aisle Window, parish church of St Neot, Cornwall, England.

John, portrayed as a younger man, is equipped with an outsize quill pen. His symbol is the rising eagle, because it was said 'his gaze pierced further into the mysteries of Heaven than that of any man'.

THE ANNUNCIATION

AND in the sixth month the angel Gabriel was sent from God unto a city of Galilee, named Nazareth, To a virgin espoused to a man whose name was Joseph, of the house of David; and the virgin's name was Mary. And the angel came in unto her, and said, Hail, thou that art highly favoured, the Lord is with thee: blessed art thou among women. And when she saw him, she was troubled at his saying, and cast in her mind what manner of salutation this should be. And the angel said unto her, Fear not, Mary: for thou hast found favour with God. And, behold, thou shalt conceive in thy womb, and bring forth a son, and shalt call his name JESUS. He shall be great, and shall be called the Son of the Highest: and the Lord God shall give unto him the throne of his father David: And he shall reign over the house of Jacob for ever; and of his kingdom there shall be no end. Then said Mary unto the angel, How shall this be, seeing I know not a man? And the angel answered and said unto her, The Holy Ghost shall come upon thee, and the power of the Highest shall overshadow thee: therefore also that holy thing which shall be born of thee shall be called the Son of God. And, behold, thy cousin Elisabeth, she hath also conceived a son in her old age: and this is the sixth month with her, who was called barren. For with God nothing shall be impossible. And Mary said, Behold the handmaid of the Lord; be it unto me according to thy word. And the angel departed from her.

LUKE
Chapter 1:26–38

The Annunciation
Window by Edward Burne-Jones in the Chapel, Castle Howard, Yorkshire, England; 1874.

A richly-robed angel makes the sign of blessing, while a haloed white dove (symbolizing the Holy Spirit), a coronet of fire around its throat, flies towards Mary. The shrub represents the Tree of Life; down its stem a human-headed serpent, Satan, falls.

The Visitation
Panel in the fourteenth-century Smiths' Window in the North Aisle of Freiburg-im-Breisgau Cathedral, Southern Germany.

Mary is portrayed, as traditionally, dressed in blue. Elizabeth, already pregnant, lays one hand on Mary's stomach, to show that Mary has told her of the angel's visit, the other on her shoulder to reassure her.

The journey to Bethlehem
Window in Notre-Dame-en-Vaux, Châlons-sur-Marne, France; 1527.

This window catches the eye not only with its beauty, but also with its obvious patches. Repairs have been effected with glass that matches for colour or size, but which often features detail irrelevant to the overall design. For instance, Mary's long golden hair, falling over her left shoulder, is in fact part of a scroll border cut to replace a damaged section in this window. Similarly the forelegs of the oxen are now represented by a patch illustrating brickwork. The original artist has included interesting details, such as the fortified gateway with its portcullis raised, and the tubs protecting the tree bark from the ravages of goats.

The Nativity
Fifteenth-century window, believed to be by Pedro Bonifacio, in a chapel in Toledo Cathedral, Spain.

Two lancets and a quatrefoil above illustrate the angels, the shepherds, and the adoration of Joseph and Mary. Mary, robed in her traditional colours, has a halo and a circlet of pearls around her head. In the quatrefoil (*above*), the infant Jesus is pictured holding either an orb (but no sceptre) or a golden apple, the latter sometimes symbolizing his role as the Second Adam. Unusually, the medieval artist's name is known to us.

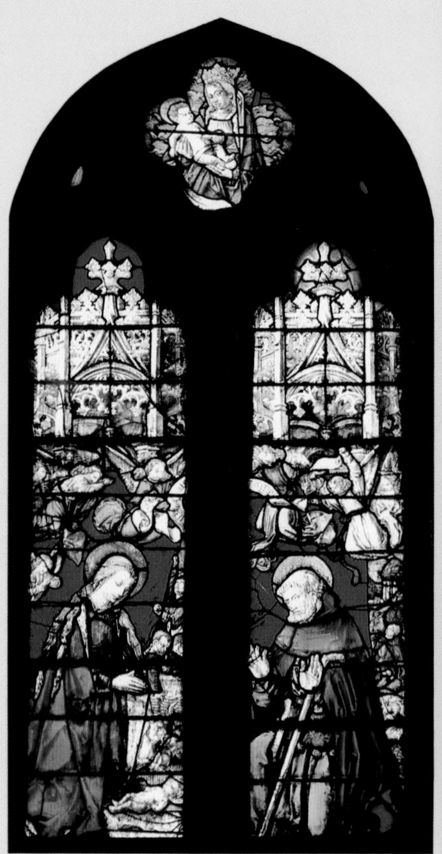

THE NATIVITY — LUKE Chapter 2:1–7

AND it came to pass in those days, that there went out a decree from Caesar Augustus, that all the world should be taxed. (And this taxing was first made when Cyrenius was governor of Syria.) And all went to be taxed, every one into his own city. And Joseph also went up from Galilee, out of the city of Nazareth, into Judaea, unto the city of David, which is called Bethlehem; (because he was of the house and lineage of David:) To be taxed with Mary his espoused wife, being great with child. And so it was, that, while they were there, the days were accomplished that she should be delivered. And she brought forth her firstborn son, and wrapped him in swaddling clothes, and laid him in a manger; because there was no room for them in the inn.

The Nativity
Lunette by Paolo Uccello in the dome of Florence Cathedral, Italy; 1443/4.

In this window, the leads have to sustain the weight of the glass and the buffeting of the elements; hence the large number of fine leads, intricately cobwebbed, and the strong cast-iron horizontal and vertical bars dividing up the artist's design into sometimes unfortunate sections. However, the fine lead is not easily seen from ground-level. Close-up, the baby Jesus can be seen to have an adult's head and hair, and the manger uniquely to be full of green cattle feed. The window is notable for its brilliant flat colour.

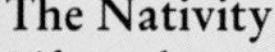

The Nativity
Fifteenth-century window by Hans Acker, Ulm Cathedral, Germany.

Acker has achieved a strikingly simple treatment within one small vertical panel. Notice the two warships, each flying a 'pennoncelle', or long, streamer-like pennant above the high poops and aft decking; the angel appearing to the shepherd; and the strong withe walls and straw roof of the stable.

The adoration of the shepherds ▷
Fifteenth-century East Window from St Peter Mancroft Church, Norwich, Norfolk, England.

This window is interesting for its unusual detail, its busy-ness and its varying scales. A diminutive midwife warms clothes by a brazier, while Mary is about to feed the baby Jesus. Joseph is portrayed as an elderly and apparently chilly man in a low armchair beside a meagre fire. The top third of the window has been clumsily repaired with unconnected scraps of glass; fortunately, the multiple star, representing the Twelve Tribes of Israel, survives unscathed. The shepherds play medieval musical instruments: horn, pipe, and twin flute.

The annunciation to the shepherds
Sixteenth-century window at Notre-Dame-en-Vaux, Châlons-sur-Marne, France.

This window exemplifies well the artist's skill in simplifying and presenting a complex narrative. The ram, ewe and lamb in the foreground echo symbolically the Holy Family. The shepherd addressed by the angel bears a staff with a paddle-like end, probably for guiding or separating sheep. The scene is set within a rural landscape with a beamed cottage and sheepfold.

LUKE
Chapter 2:8–20

THE ADORATION OF THE SHEPHERDS

AND there were in the same country shepherds abiding in the field, keeping watch over their flock by night. And, lo, the angel of the Lord came upon them, and the glory of the Lord shone round about them: and they were sore afraid. And the angel said unto them, Fear not: for, behold, I bring you good tidings of great joy, which shall be to all people. For unto you is born this day in the city of David a Saviour, which is Christ the Lord. And this shall be a sign unto you; Ye shall find the babe wrapped in swaddling clothes, lying in a manger. And suddenly there was with the angel a multitude of the heavenly host praising God, and saying, Glory to God in the highest, and on earth peace, good will toward men. And it came to pass, as the angels were gone away from them into heaven, the shepherds said one to another, Let us now go even unto Bethlehem, and see this thing which is come to pass, which the Lord hath made known unto us. And they came with haste, and found Mary, and Joseph, and the babe lying in a manger. And when they had seen it, they made known abroad the saying which was told them concerning this child. And all they that heard it wondered at those things which were told them by the shepherds. But Mary kept all these things, and pondered them in her heart. And the shepherds returned, glorifying and praising God for all the things that they had heard and seen, as it was told unto them.

The adoration of the Magi ▷
From the Bible Window No.1, in the Chapel of the Magi, Cologne Cathedral, Germany; 1250-60.

This is the oldest window in Cologne Cathedral, and, appropriately for a cathedral containing a shrine and relics of the Three Kings, portrays the Magi. As habitually in medieval iconography, the Magi are shown as of disparate ages. Mary, here given a crown, looks slightly askance at the gifts of the Magi; perhaps because she associates myrrh with the embalming of the dead. The infant Jesus holds a sceptre in his left hand, while making a sign of blessing with his right. An eight-pointed star, symbol of regeneration, is found in the border (*above left*).

The Magi
Panel from the thirteenth-century Poor Man's Bible Window, North Choir Aisle, Canterbury Cathedral, Kent, England.

The wise men appear to have brought their horses up short, and show by their different gestures their reactions to the star. Their horses are portrayed with fetlocks, which have been bred out of most twentieth-century horses.

MATTHEW
Chapter 2:1–11

THE MAGI

NOW when Jesus was born in Bethlehem of Judaea in the days of Herod the king, behold, there came wise men from the east to Jerusalem, Saying, Where is he that is born King of the Jews? for we have seen his star in the east, and are come to worship him. When Herod the king had heard these things, he was troubled, and all Jerusalem with him. And when he had gathered all the chief priests and scribes of the people together, he demanded of them where Christ should be born. And they said unto him, In Bethlehem of Judaea: for thus it is written by the prophet, And thou Bethlehem, in the land of Juda, art not the least among the princes of Juda: for out of thee shall come a Governor, that shall rule my people Israel. Then Herod, when he had privily called the wise men, inquired of them diligently what time the star appeared. And he sent them to Bethlehem, and said, Go and search diligently for the young child; and when ye have found him, bring me word again, that I may come and worship him also. When they had heard the king, they departed; and, lo, the star, which they saw in the east, went before them, till it came and stood over where the young child was. When they saw the star, they rejoiced with exceeding great joy.

And when they were come into the house, they saw the young child with Mary his mother, and fell down, and worshipped him: and when they had opened their treasures, they presented unto him gifts; gold, and frankincense, and myrrh.

MATTHEW
Chapter 2:12–18

AND being warned of God in a dream that they should not return to Herod, they departed into their own country another way. And when they were departed, behold, the angel of the Lord appeareth to Joseph in a dream, saying, Arise, and take the young child and his mother, and flee into Egypt, and be thou there until I bring thee word: for Herod will seek the young child to destroy him. When he arose, he took the young child and his mother by night, and departed into Egypt: And was there until the death of Herod: that it might be fulfilled which was spoken of the Lord by the prophet, saying, Out of Egypt have I called my son.

Then Herod, when he saw that he was mocked of the wise men, was exceeding wroth, and sent forth, and slew all the children that were in Bethlehem, and in all the coasts thereof, from two years old and under, according to the time which he had diligently inquired of the wise men. Then was fulfilled that which was spoken by Jeremy the prophet, saying, In Rama was there a voice heard, lamentation, and weeping, and great mourning, Rachel weeping for her children, and would not be comforted, because they are not.

The dream of the Magi
A Roundel in the Poor Man's Bible Window No.1, in the North Choir Aisle, Canterbury Cathedral, Kent, England.

The richly-dressed kings are sleeping in their crowns, which aids their identification. They rest on a large couch with wooden feet.

The slaughter of the innocents
Sixteenth-century window in the Church of Notre-Dame-en-Vaux, Châlons-sur-Marne, France.

The differing costumes of the women in this terrible scene reflect their varied social status; Herod had ordered the killing of *all* Jewish male babies. Pagan temples are seen in the background.

The flight into Egypt
Fourteenth-century window in Freiburg-im-Breisgau Cathedral, Germany.

In this unusual design the focus is on the main figures, and background detail is omitted in favour of a lozenge pattern. Joseph is portrayed cleanshaven and younger than normal; his concern for mother and baby is shown not only by his leading the donkey on which Mary rides side-saddle, but also by his lending her his cloak and carrying the packs.

MATTHEW
Chapter 2:19–23

But when Herod was dead, behold, an angel of the Lord appeareth in a dream to Joseph in Egypt, Saying, Arise, and take the young child and his mother, and go into the land of Israel: for they are dead which sought the young child's life. And he arose, and took the young child and his mother, and came into the land of Israel. But when he heard that Archelaus did reign in Judaea in the room of his father Herod, he was afraid to go thither: notwithstanding, being warned of God in a dream, he turned aside into the parts of Galilee: And he came and dwelt in a city called Nazareth: that it might be fulfilled which was spoken by the prophets, He shall be called a Nazarene.

Jesus the boy carpenter
Seventeenth-century Dutch roundel; now in Nowton Church, Suffolk, England.

The Holy Family in Joseph's carpenter's workshop. Mary is depicted conventionally sitting sewing. The carpenter's tools are, of course, typical of seventeenth-century Holland.

ELIZABETH AND JOHN

Now Elisabeth's full time came that she should be delivered; and she brought forth a son. And her neighbours and her cousins heard how the Lord had shewed great mercy upon her; and they rejoiced with her. And it came to pass, that on the eighth day they came to circumcise the child; and they called him Zacharias, after the name of his father. And his mother answered and said, Not so; but he shall be called John. And they said unto her, There is none of thy kindred that is called by this name. And they made signs to his father, how he would have him called. And he asked for a writing table, and wrote, saying, His name is John. And they marvelled all. And his mouth was opened immediately, and his tongue loosed, and he spake, and praised God.

LUKE
Chapter 1:57–64

The Virgin and Child
Detail from the fourteenth-century East Window, Church of St Michael and All Angels, Eaton Bishop, Herefordshire, England.

This window is outstanding in its expression of Mary's relaxed, supple posture and for the empathy between mother and child. Mary holds a formalized lily in her right hand; the child a fledgling bird, stained yellow.

Elizabeth and John the Baptist
Window by Edward Burne-Jones in St Martin's Church, Brampton, Cumbria; 1888.

Elizabeth, John's mother, is depicted as old, her head bent, eyes straining to read from the illuminated book. The young John carries a bowl, prefiguring his role as baptizer, and stands on the opposite bank of a stream, which signifies the river Jordan, where he was to baptize Jesus.

AND when he was twelve years old, they went up to Jerusalem after the custom of the feast. And when they had fulfilled the days, as they returned, the child Jesus tarried behind in Jerusalem; and Joseph and his mother knew not of it. But they, supposing him to have been in the company, went a day's journey; and they sought him among their kinsfolk and acquaintance. And when they found him not, they turned back again to Jerusalem, seeking him. And it came to pass, that after three days they found him in the temple, sitting in the midst of the doctors, both hearing them, and asking them questions. And all that heard him were astonished at his understanding and answers. And when they saw him, they were amazed: and his mother said unto him, Son, why hast thou thus dealt with us? behold, thy father and I have sought thee sorrowing. And he said unto them, How is it that ye sought me? wist ye not that I must be about my Father's business? And they understood not the saying which he spake unto them. And he went down with them, and came to Nazareth, and was subject unto them: but his mother kept all these sayings in her heart. And Jesus increased in wisdom and stature, and in favour with God and man.

LUKE
Chapter 2:42–52

The young Jesus disputes with the priests
Detail from Window 13, St John's Church, Gouda, The Netherlands; 1560.

The artist shows the old priests checking the Jewish Law in their books, while the young Jesus counts off his points on his fingers. The chequered effect on the clothing is due to wire-netting fitted outside the church to protect the glass, and is no part of the artist's original design.

The baptism of Jesus
Nineteenth-century window by Edward Burne-Jones at the Church of All Hallows, Allerton, Liverpool, England.

The window consists of three tall, slim lights below floral tracery. John the Baptist (*left*) holds a bowl of water preparatory to the baptism; an angel (*right*) holds Jesus' discarded blue outer robe. The dove of the Holy Spirit, descending on Jesus (*centre*), bears a flash of red in its beak.

MARK
Chapter 1:9–11

JESUS IS BAPTIZED

AND it came to pass in those days, that Jesus came from Nazareth of Galilee, and was baptized of John in Jordan. And straightway coming up out of the water, he saw the heavens opened, and the Spirit like a dove descending upon him: And there came a voice from heaven, saying, Thou art my beloved Son, in whom I am well pleased.

JESUS IS TEMPTED

THEN was Jesus led up of the Spirit into the wilderness to be tempted of the devil. And when he had fasted forty days and forty nights, he was afterward an hungred. And when the tempter came to him, he said, If thou be the Son of God, command that these stones be made bread. But he answered and said, It is written, Man shall not live by bread alone, but by every word that proceedeth out of the mouth of God.

MATTHEW
Chapter 4:1–4

The first temptation of Christ
Originally from Troyes Cathedral, France; now in the Victoria and Albert Museum, London, England; *c*1170.

There is no mistaking the devil in this medieval portrayal, where he is shown as a green-skinned creature, with blue serpents emerging from his head, and with winged heels and strange blue-winged hips. He holds a huge stone. Jesus holds a book, signifying his reply to the tempter, 'It is written...'.

The second temptation of Christ
Originally in Troyes Cathedral, France; now in the Victoria and Albert Museum, London, England; *c.*1170.

The Temple is here represented by a tower-like structure, incorporating elaborate wrought-iron scroll-work. Satan is carrying Jesus in his arms to the 'pinnacle' of the Temple, as described in the Gospels. Again Jesus is shown bearing a book, signifying his reliance on Scripture.

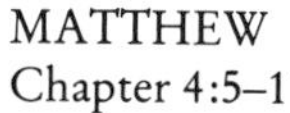

MATTHEW
Chapter 4:5–11

THEN the devil taketh him up into the holy city, and setteth him on a pinnacle of the temple, And saith unto him, If thou be the Son of God, cast thyself down: for it is written, He shall give his angels charge concerning thee: and in their hands they shall bear thee up, lest at any time thou dash thy foot against a stone. Jesus said unto him, It is written again, Thou shalt not tempt the Lord thy God. Again, the devil taketh him up into an exceeding high mountain, and sheweth him all the kingdoms of the world, and the glory of them; And saith unto him, All these things will I give thee, if thou wilt fall down and worship me. Then saith Jesus unto him, Get thee hence, Satan: for it is written, Thou shalt worship the Lord thy God, and him only shalt thou serve. Then the devil leaveth him, and, behold, angels came and ministered unto him.

MATTHEW
Chapter 4:17–25

The calling of Peter and Andrew
Twentieth-century window by Gabriel Loire, Lèves, France.

A scene full of urgency and action. The brothers' spontaneous response to Jesus' call is reflected in the abandoned catch of fish, the sheet left loose in the boat and the watching fellow fishermen.

JESUS BEGINS TO PREACH

FROM that time Jesus began to preach, and to say, Repent: for the kingdom of heaven is at hand.

And Jesus, walking by the sea of Galilee, saw two brethren, Simon called Peter, and Andrew his brother, casting a net into the sea: for they were fishers. And he saith unto them, Follow me, and I will make you fishers of men. And they straightway left their nets, and followed him. And going on from thence, he saw other two brethren, James the son of Zebedee, and John his brother, in a ship with Zebedee their father, mending their nets; and he called them. And they immediately left the ship and their father, and followed him.

And Jesus went about all Galilee, teaching in their synagogues, and preaching the gospel of the kingdom, and healing all manner of sickness and all manner of disease among the people. And his fame went throughout all Syria: and they brought unto him all sick people that were taken with divers diseases and torments, and those which were possessed with devils, and those which were lunatick, and those that had the palsy; and he healed them. And there followed him great multitudes of people from Galilee, and from Decapolis, and from Jerusalem, and from Judaea, and from beyond Jordan.

Stilling the storm
Fifteenth-century panel in the Chapel of the Holy Sacrament, Cologne Cathedral, Germany.

There is a marked contrast between the calm face of Christ and the tense fear of most of the Apostles. Notice the nautical details such as the pulleys outboard, the 'spearhead' metal fastenings of the stays and the reefing of the sail. The tawny streaks on the sail are due to the melting of resin-glue applied in earlier centuries to repair cracks in the glass.

THE SERMON ON THE MOUNT

AND seeing the multitudes, he went up into a mountain: and when he was set, his disciples came unto him: And he opened his mouth, and taught them, saying, Blessed are the poor in spirit: for theirs is the kingdom of heaven. Blessed are they that mourn: for they shall be comforted. Blessed are the meek: for they shall inherit the earth. Blessed are they which do hunger and thirst after righteousness: for they shall be filled. Blessed are the merciful: for they shall obtain mercy. Blessed are the pure in heart: for they shall see God. Blessed are the peacemakers: for they shall be called the children of God. Blessed are they which are persecuted for righteousness' sake: for theirs is the kingdom of heaven. Blessed are ye, when men shall revile you, and persecute you, and shall say all manner of evil against you falsely, for my sake. Rejoice, and be exceeding glad: for great is your reward in heaven: for so persecuted they the prophets which were before you.

Ye are the salt of the earth: but if the salt have lost his savour, wherewith shall it be salted? it is thenceforth good for nothing, but to be cast out, and to be trodden under foot of men. Ye are the light of the world. A city that is set on an hill cannot be hid. Neither do men light a candle, and put it under a bushel, but on a candlestick; and it giveth light unto all that are in the house. Let your light so shine before men, that they may see your good works, and glorify your Father which is in heaven.

Think not that I am come to destroy the law, or the prophets: I am not come to destroy, but to fulfil. For verily I say unto you, Till heaven and earth pass, one jot or one tittle shall in no wise pass from the law, till all be fulfilled. Whosoever therefore shall break one of these least commandments, and shall teach men so, he shall be called the least in the kingdom of heaven: but whosoever shall do and teach them, the same shall be called great in the kingdom of heaven. For I say unto you, That except your righteousness shall exceed the righteousness of the scribes and Pharisees, ye shall in no case enter into the kingdom of heaven.

Ye have heard that it was said by them of old time, Thou shalt not kill; and whosoever shall kill shall be in danger of the judgment: But I say unto you, That whosoever is angry with his brother without a cause shall be in danger of the judgment: and whosoever shall say to his brother, Raca, shall be in danger of the council: but whosoever shall say, Thou fool, shall be in danger of hell fire. Therefore if thou bring thy gift to the altar, and there rememberest that thy brother hath ought against thee; Leave there thy gift before the altar, and go thy way; first be reconciled to thy brother, and then come and offer thy gift. Agree with thine adversary quickly, whiles thou art in the way with him; lest at any time the adversary deliver thee to the judge, and the judge deliver thee to the officer, and thou be cast into prison. Verily I say unto thee, Thou shalt by no means come out thence, till thou hast paid the uttermost farthing.

Ye have heard that it was said by them of old time, Thou shalt not commit adultery: But I say unto you, That whosoever looketh on a woman to lust after her hath committed adultery with her already in his heart. And

The Sermon on the Mount
Nineteenth-century window in the Church of St Peter Mancroft, Norwich, Norfolk, England

A clear and simple design from the Norwich School of glass painting and glazing. The artist includes children as well as men and women in the crowd listening to Jesus, and shows a distinct sadness in Jesus' eyes.

if thy right eye offend thee, pluck it out, and cast it from thee: for it is profitable for thee that one of thy members should perish, and not that thy whole body should be cast into hell. And if thy right hand offend thee, cut it off, and cast it from thee: for it is profitable for thee that one of thy members should perish, and not that thy whole body should be cast into hell. It hath been said, Whosoever shall put away his wife, let him give her a writing of divorcement: But I say unto you, That whosoever shall put away his wife, saving for the cause of fornication, causeth her to commit adultery: and whosoever shall marry her that is divorced committeth adultery.

THE MARRIAGE AT CANA

AND the third day there was a marriage in Cana of Galilee; and the mother of Jesus was there: And both Jesus was called, and his disciples, to the marriage. And when they wanted wine, the mother of Jesus saith unto him, They have no wine. Jesus saith unto her, Woman, what have I to do with thee? mine hour is not yet come. His mother saith unto the servants, Whatsoever he saith unto you, do it. And there were set there six waterpots of stone, after the manner of the purifying of the Jews, containing two or three firkins apiece. Jesus saith unto them, Fill the waterpots with water. And they filled them up to the brim. And he saith unto them, Draw out now, and bear unto the governor of the feast. And they bare it. When the ruler of the feast had tasted the water that was made wine, and knew not whence it was: (but the servants which drew the water knew;) the governor of the feast called the bridegroom, And saith unto him, Every man at the beginning doth set forth good wine; and when men have well drunk, then that which is worse: but thou hast kept the good wine until now. This beginning of miracles did Jesus in Cana of Galilee, and manifested forth his glory; and his disciples believed on him.

JOHN
Chapter 2:1–11

The marriage at Cana
Roundel in the thirteenth-century Poor Man's Bible Window No.2 in the North Choir Aisle, Canterbury Cathedral, Kent, England.

This roundel catches the moment when Jesus makes a sign with his right hand to effect the miraculous change of the water into wine. One youth bears aloft a jar, perhaps to show the quality of the new wine to the guests. There are no drinking cups or goblets on the table, which is laden with fish, fowl, a pomegranate and an artichoke.

JESUS FEEDS FIVE THOUSAND

One of his disciples, Andrew, Simon Peter's brother, saith unto him, There is a lad here, which hath five barley loaves, and two small fishes: but what are they among so many? And Jesus said, Make the men sit down. Now there was much grass in the place. So the men sat down, in number about five thousand. And Jesus took the loaves; and when he had given thanks, he distributed to the disciples, and the disciples to them that were set down; and likewise of the fishes as much as they would. When they were filled, he said unto his disciples, Gather up the fragments that remain, that nothing be lost. Therefore they gathered them together, and filled twelve baskets with the fragments of the five barley loaves, which remained over and above unto them that had eaten.

JOHN
Chapter 6:8–13

Feeding the five thousand
Detail from a sixteenth-century window in the Church of St Pierre, Dreux, France.

Notice the artist's attention to facial expression: among the crowd we can find puzzlement, aggression, disbelief, the crooked mouth of the whisperer, a grateful woman, and a critical priest. The loaves and fish are very large considering they originally constituted a boy's lunch!

Christ feeding the five thousand
From Troyes Cathedral, France; now in the Victoria and Albert Museum, London; 1223.

JESUS HEALS A BLIND MAN

AND he cometh to Bethsaida; and they bring a blind man unto him, and besought him to touch him. And he took the blind man by the hand, and led him out of the town; and when he had spit on his eyes, and put his hands upon him, he asked him if he saw ought. And he looked up, and said, I see men as trees, walking. After that he put his hands again upon his eyes, and made him look up: and he was restored, and saw every man clearly.

MARK
Chapter 8:22–25

Christ heals a blind man at Bethsaida
Nineteenth-century window from Lancaster, Lancashire, England.

Although the lead used in this window is heavy, the details in the glass are finely drawn, and the strength and clarity is not lost. Notice Christ's distinctive decorated halo.

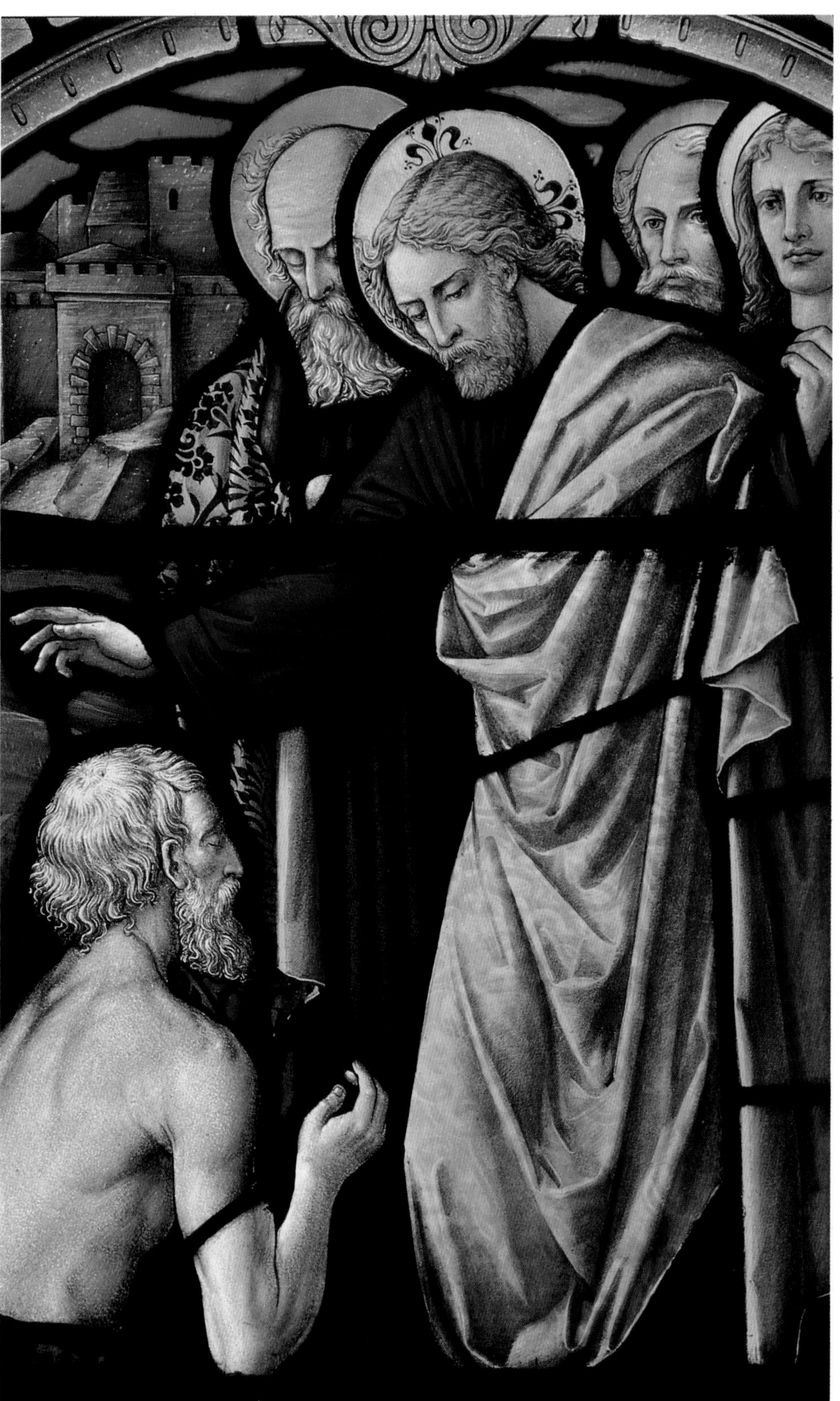

MATTHEW
Chapter 14:22–33

Peter tries to walk on the water
Small Swiss panel by Johann Caspar Herman, now in Darmstadt Museum, Germany; 1643.

Six severe cracks in the glass have been heavily glued, and the glue has turned black with the passing of time. The apostles' boat appears to be dismasted, perhaps symbolizing their lack of direction without Jesus.

JESUS WALKS ON THE SEA

AND straightway Jesus constrained his disciples to get into a ship, and to go before him unto the other side, while he sent the multitudes away. And when he had sent the multitudes away, he went up into a mountain apart to pray: and when the evening was come, he was there alone. But the ship was now in the midst of the sea, tossed with waves: for the wind was contrary. And in the fourth watch of the night Jesus went unto them, walking on the sea. And when the disciples saw him walking on the sea, they were troubled, saying, It is a spirit; and they cried out for fear. But straightway Jesus spake unto them, saying, Be of good cheer; it is I; be not afraid. And Peter answered him and said, Lord, if it be thou, bid me come unto thee on the water. And he said, Come. And when Peter was come down out of the ship, he walked on the water, to go to Jesus. But when he saw the wind boisterous, he was afraid; and beginning to sink, he cried, saying, Lord, save me. And immediately Jesus stretched forth his hand, and caught him, and said unto him, O thou of little faith, wherefore didst thou doubt? And when they were come into the ship, the wind ceased. Then they that were in the ship came and worshipped him, saying, Of a truth thou art the Son of God.

The parable of the lost sheep
Nineteenth-century window in St Nicholas' Church, Hillesden, Buckinghamshire, England.

The shepherd returns to the withe sheepfold with the lost sheep across his shoulders, and is greeted joyously by an old man. The dog has evidently been searching wearily with the shepherd; its tongue hangs out thirstily!

LUKE
Chapter 15:1–32

JESUS' PARABLES

THEN drew near unto him all the publicans and sinners for to hear him. And the Pharisees and scribes murmured, saying, This man receiveth sinners, and eateth with them.

And he spake this parable unto them, saying, What man of you, having an hundred sheep, if he lose one of them, doth not leave the ninety and nine in the wilderness, and go after that which is lost, until he find it? And when he hath found it, he layeth it on his shoulders, rejoicing. And when he cometh home, he calleth together his friends and neighbours, saying unto them, Rejoice with me; for I have found my sheep which was lost. I say unto you, that likewise joy shall be in heaven over one sinner that repenteth, more than over ninety and nine just persons, which need no repentance.

Either what woman having ten pieces of silver, if she lose one piece, doth not light a candle, and sweep the house, and seek diligently till she find it? And when she hath found it, she calleth her friends and her neighbours together, saying, Rejoice with me; for I have found the piece which I had lost. Likewise, I say unto you, there is joy in the presence of the angels of God over one sinner that repenteth.

And he said, A certain man had two sons: And the younger of them said to his father, Father, give me the portion of goods that falleth to me. And he divided unto them his living. And not many days after the younger son gathered all together, and took his journey into a far country, and there wasted his substance with riotous living. And when he had spent all, there arose a mighty famine in that land; and he began to be in want. And he went and joined himself to a citizen of that country; and he sent him into his fields to feed swine. And he would fain have filled his belly with the husks that the swine did eat: and no man gave unto him. And when he came to himself, he said, How many hired servants of my father's have bread enough and to spare, and I perish with hunger! I will arise and go to my

The parable of the dragnet
Nineteenth-century window in St Nicholas' Church, Hillesden, Buckinghamshire, England.

Note the huge variety of fish caught in the net; they include eels, flying-fish, catfish, mackerel and flatfish.

POENITENTIA.
Es ist mir gůt das du mich demůtigist.
PSALM: 119.
O Gott biß mir sünder gnedig.
LVCÆ. 18 Cap.

The prodigal son
Small panel by Christoph Murer; now in the Tucher Haus Museum, Nuremberg, Germany; 1610.

The artist has striven to portray the prodigal's poverty and dejection at the nadir of his fortunes, in contrast to the contentment of the well-fed swine.

The return of the prodigal son
Nineteenth-century window in St Nicholas' Church, Hillesden, Buckinghamshire, England.

The window shows interesting details of a Victorian swineherd's life. For instance the piglets are feeding at a separate tub from the grown swine. The farm is in poor repair. The two contrasting panels, depicting the swineherd's life and the father's house, show the choice facing the prodigal.

father, and will say unto him, Father, I have sinned against heaven, and before thee, And am no more worthy to be called thy son: make me as one of thy hired servants. And he arose, and came to his father. But when he was yet a great way off, his father saw him, and had compassion, and ran, and fell on his neck, and kissed him. And the son said unto him, Father, I have sinned against heaven, and in thy sight, and am no more worthy to be called thy son. But the father said to his servants, Bring forth the best robe, and put it on him; and put a ring on his hand, and shoes on his feet: And bring hither the fatted calf, and kill it; and let us eat, and be merry: For this my son was dead, and is alive again; he was lost, and is found. And they began to be merry. Now his elder son was in the field: and as he came and drew nigh to the house, he heard musick and dancing. And he called one of the servants, and asked what these things meant. And he said unto him, Thy brother is come; and thy father hath killed the fatted calf, because he hath received him safe and sound. And he was angry, and would not go in: therefore came his father out, and intreated him. And he answering said to his father, Lo, these many years do I serve thee, neither transgressed I at any time thy commandment: and yet thou never gavest me a kid, that I might make merry with my friends: But as soon as this thy son was come, which hath devoured thy living with harlots, thou hast killed for him the fatted calf. And he said unto him, Son, thou art ever with me, and all that I have is thine. It was meet that we should make merry, and be glad: for this thy brother was dead, and is alive again; and was lost, and is found.

The parable of the Good Samaritan
Detail from a window in the Church of St Margaret and St Andrew, Littleham, Devon, England.

This detail depicts the brigands lying in wait for the innocent young traveller, who is shown equipped with a staff and scrip, or purse. The waiting thieves are well-armed, and clearly anticipate a good haul!

THE GOOD SAMARITAN

LUKE
Chapter 10:25–37

AND, behold, a certain lawyer stood up, and tempted him, saying, Master, what shall I do to inherit eternal life? He said unto him, What is written in the law? how readest thou? And he answering said, Thou shalt love the Lord thy God with all thy heart, and with all thy soul, and with all thy strength, and with all thy mind; and thy neighbour as thyself. And he said unto him, Thou hast answered right: this do, and thou shalt live. But he, willing to justify himself, said unto Jesus, And who is my neighbour? And Jesus answering said, A certain man went down from Jerusalem to Jericho, and fell among thieves, which stripped him of his raiment, and wounded him, and departed, leaving him half dead. And by chance there came down a certain priest that way: and when he saw him, he passed by on the other side. And likewise a Levite, when he was at the place, came and looked on him, and passed by on the other side. But a certain Samaritan, as he journeyed, came where he was: and when he saw him, he had compassion on him, And went to him, and bound up his wounds, pouring in oil and wine, and set him on his own beast, and brought him to an inn, and took care of him. And on the morrow when he departed, he took out two pence, and gave them to the host, and said unto him, Take care of him; and whatsoever thou spendest more, when I come again, I will repay thee. Which now of these three, thinkest thou, was neighbour unto him that fell among the thieves? And he said, He that shewed mercy on him. Then said Jesus unto him, Go, and do thou likewise.

The parable of the Good Samaritan
Detail from the thirteenth-century Good Samaritan Window in the South Aisle of Chartres Cathedral, France.

This single panel is a quatrefoil design of small scenes, with a vivid centrepiece of two brigands or robbers, one of whom is straining a crossbow into the firing position. In the right-hand section the Samaritan is trying to rescue the traveller, who is still being beaten by the thieves. The panel was donated by the Guild of Shoemakers, who are depicted at their trade at the base of the panel.

MATTHEW
Chapter 13:1–32

THE SOWER

THE same day went Jesus out of the house, and sat by the sea side. And great multitudes were gathered together unto him, so that he went into a ship, and sat; and the whole multitude stood on the shore. And he spake many things unto them in parables, saying, Behold, a sower went forth to sow; And when he sowed, some seeds fell by the way side, and the fowls came and devoured them up: Some fell upon stony places, where they had not much earth: and forthwith they sprung up, because they had no deepness of earth: And when the sun was up, they were scorched; and because they had no root, they withered away. And some fell among thorns; and the thorns sprung up, and choked them: But other fell into good ground, and brought forth fruit, some an hundredfold, some sixtyfold, some thirtyfold. Who hath ears to hear, let him hear. And the disciples came, and said unto him, Why speakest thou unto them in parables? He answered and said unto them, Because it is given unto you to know the mysteries of the kingdom of heaven, but to them it is not given. For whosoever hath, to him shall be given, and he shall have more abundance: but whosoever hath not, from him shall be taken away even that he hath. Therefore speak I to them in parables: because they seeing see not; and hearing they hear not, neither do they understand. And in them is fulfilled the prophecy of Esaias, which saith, By hearing ye shall hear, and shall not understand; and seeing ye shall see, and shall not perceive: For this people's heart is waxed gross, and their ears are dull of hearing, and their eyes they have closed; lest at any time they should see with their eyes, and hear with their ears, and should understand with their heart, and should be converted, and I should heal them. But blessed are your eyes, for they see: and your ears, for they hear. For verily I say unto you, That many prophets and righteous men have desired to see those things which ye see, and have not seen them; and to hear those things which ye hear, and have not heard them.

Hear ye therefore the parable of the sower. When any one heareth the word of the kingdom, and understandeth it not, then cometh the wicked one, and catcheth away that which was sown in his heart. This is he which received seed by the way side. But he that received the seed into stony places, the same is he that heareth the word, and anon with joy receiveth it; Yet hath he not root in himself, but dureth for a while: for when tribulation or persecution ariseth because of the word, by and by he is offended. He also that received seed among the thorns is he that heareth the word; and the care of this world, and the deceitfulness of riches, choke the word, and he becometh unfruitful. But he that received seed into the good ground is he that heareth the word, and understandeth it; which also beareth fruit, and bringeth forth, some an hundredfold, some sixty, some thirty.

Another parable put he forth unto them, saying, The kingdom of heaven is likened unto a man which sowed good seed in his field: But while men slept, his enemy came and sowed tares among the wheat, and went his way. But when the blade was sprung up, and brought forth fruit, then appeared the tares also. So the servants of the householder came and said unto him, Sir, didst not thou sow good seed in thy field? from whence then hath it

The parable of the tares
Nineteenth-century window in St Nicholas' Church, Hillesden, Buckinghamshire, England.

The tall wheat – such as is no longer grown for straw – is reaped by hand-sickle. In the foreground a fire is lit to destroy the weeds and tares. The leading in this window is light and unobtrusive.

The parable of the sower
Detail from the early thirteenth-century Poor Man's Bible Window, North Choir Aisle, Canterbury Cathedral, Kent, England.

The strength of this window lies in its simplicity. The artist portrays a medieval farmer dressed in a smock, with a basket of grain slung around his neck. He also depicts clearly the seed in the furrows and the predatory tares. The design is clearly related to the lead outlines, which help support the weight of the glass throughout the panel.

tares? He said unto them, An enemy hath done this. The servants said unto him, Wilt thou then that we go and gather them up? But he said, Nay; lest while he gather up the tares, ye root up also the wheat with them. Let both grow together until the harvest: and in the time of harvest I will say to the reapers, Gather ye together first the tares, and bind them in bundles to burn them: but gather the wheat into my barn.

Another parable put he forth unto them, saying, The kingdom of heaven is like to a grain of mustard seed, which a man took, and sowed in his field: Which indeed is the least of all seeds: but when it is grown, it is the greatest among herbs, and becometh a tree, so that the birds of the air come and lodge in the branches thereof.

THE TRANSFIGURATION

AND after six days Jesus taketh Peter, James, and John his brother, and bringeth them up into an high mountain apart, And was transfigured before them: and his face did shine as the sun, and his raiment was white as the light. And, behold, there appeared unto them Moses and Elias talking with him. Then answered Peter, and said unto Jesus, Lord, it is good for us to be here: if thou wilt, let us make here three tabernacles; one for thee, and one for Moses and one for Elias. While he yet spake, behold, a bright cloud overshadowed them: and behold a voice out of the cloud, which said, This is my beloved Son, in whom I am well pleased; hear ye him. And when the disciples heard it, they fell on their face, and were sore afraid. And Jesus came and touched them, and said, Arise, and be not afraid. And when they had lifted up their eyes, they saw no man, save Jesus only. And as they came down from the mountain, Jesus charged them, saying, Tell the vision to no man, until the Son of man be risen again from the dead. And his disciples asked him, saying, Why then say the scribes that Elias must first come? And Jesus answered and said unto them, Elias truly shall first come, and restore all things. But I say unto you, That Elias is come already, and they knew him not, but have done unto him whatsoever they listed. Likewise shall also the Son of man suffer of them. Then the disciples understood that he spake unto them of John the Baptist.

And when they were come to the multitude, there came to him a certain man, kneeling down to him, and saying, Lord, have mercy on my son: for he is lunatick, and sore vexed: for ofttimes he falleth into the fire, and oft into the water. And I brought him to thy disciples, and they could not cure him. Then Jesus answered and said, O faithless and perverse generation, how long shall I be with you? how long shall I suffer you? bring him hither to me. And Jesus rebuked the devil; and he departed out of him: and the child was cured from that very hour. Then came the disciples to Jesus apart, and said, Why could not we cast him out? And Jesus said unto them, Because of your unbelief: for verily I say unto you, If ye have faith as a grain of mustard seed, ye shall say unto this mountain, Remove hence to yonder place; and it shall remove; and nothing shall be impossible unto you. Howbeit this kind goeth not out but by prayer and fasting.

MATTHEW
Chapter 17:1–21

The Transfiguration
Sixteenth-century window in the Church of La Madeleine, Vermeuil, France.

A difficult scene to illustrate; here the artist shows the figure of Christ surrounded by rays of light, with golden rays from his mouth illuminating the book (the Word).

MARY ANOINTS JESUS' FEET

AND one of the Pharisees desired him that he would eat with him. And he went into the Pharisee's house, and sat down to meat. And, behold, a woman in the city, which was a sinner, when she knew that Jesus sat at meat in the Pharisee's house, brought an alabaster box of ointment, And stood at his feet behind him weeping, and began to wash his feet with tears, and did wipe them with the hairs of her head, and kissed his feet, and anointed them with the ointment. Now when the Pharisee which had bidden him saw it, he spake within himself, saying, This man, if he were a prophet, would have known who and what manner of woman this is that toucheth him: for she is a sinner. And Jesus answering said unto him, Simon, I have somewhat to say unto thee. And he saith, Master, say on. There was a certain creditor which had two debtors: the one owed five hundred pence, and the other fifty. And when they had nothing to pay, he frankly forgave them both. Tell me therefore, which of them will love him most? Simon answered and said, I suppose that he, to whom he forgave most. And he said unto him, Thou hast rightly judged. And he turned to the woman, and said unto Simon, Seest thou this woman? I entered into thine house, thou gavest me no water for my feet: but she hath washed my feet with tears, and wiped them with the hairs of her head. Thou gavest me no kiss: but this woman since the time I came in hath not ceased to kiss my feet. My head with oil thou didst not anoint: but this woman hath anointed my feet with ointment. Wherefore I say unto thee, Her sins, which are many, are forgiven; for she loved much: but to whom little is forgiven, the same loveth little. And he said unto her, Thy sins are forgiven. And they that sat at meat with him began to say within themselves, Who is this that forgiveth sins also? And he said to the woman, Thy faith hath saved thee; go in peace.

LUKE
Chapter 7:36–50

Jesus and the woman caught in adultery
A window by Guillaume de Marcillat, Arezzo Cathedral, Italy; 1519–24.

In this instance, two tall lights form a single scene. The Temple is portrayed as an ornate, marbled structure, thronged with men from every walk of life. A venerable, richly-robed man turns away as Jesus admonishes the woman, who stands demure, dressed in a velvet gown with the pleated apron characteristic of the rich bourgeoisie of the sixteenth century. Perhaps the lettered stone block at Jesus' feet is intended to represent Jesus' writing on the Temple floor.

Mary Magdalene anoints Jesus' feet
A Flemish panel in the Church of Llanwenllwyfo, Anglesey, North Wales.

The supper table is shown as simply laid with beakers, knives, platters and a salt cellar, and with fish and bread rolls to eat. Nothing is allowed to distract from the figures of Mary Magdalene, with her extraordinarily long hair, and Jesus.

POSVERVT·A
VERSVM
ME·MALA
PRO BONI

THE TRIUMPHAL ENTRY

AND it came to pass, when he was come nigh to Bethphage and Bethany, at the mount called the mount of Olives, he sent two of his disciples, Saying, Go ye into the village over against you; in the which at your entering ye shall find a colt tied, whereon yet never man sat: loose him, and bring him hither. And if any man ask you, Why do ye loose him? thus shall ye say unto him, Because the Lord hath need of him. And they that were sent went their way, and found even as he had said unto them. And as they were loosing the colt, the owners thereof said unto them, Why loose ye the colt? And they said, The Lord hath need of him. And they brought him to Jesus: and they cast their garments upon the colt, and they set Jesus thereon. And as he went, they spread their clothes in the way. And when he was come nigh, even now at the descent of the mount of Olives, the whole multitude of the disciples began to rejoice and praise God with a loud voice for all the mighty works that they had seen; Saying, Blessed be the King that cometh in the name of the Lord: peace in heaven, and glory in the highest. And some of the Pharisees from among the multitude said unto him, Master, rebuke thy disciples. And he answered and said unto them, I tell you that, if these should hold their peace, the stones would immediately cry out.

LUKE
Chapter 19:29–40

The triumphal entry into Jerusalem
Detail from a fifteenth-century window by Hans Acker in the Besserer Chapel, Ulm Cathedral, Germany.

Hans Acker, a past-master at compact illustration, includes much detail mentioned in the biblical account, but not at the expense of clear overall design. Notice the man watching from a tree, and the metal-bound money casket.

The entry into Jerusalem
Detail from the fourteenth-century Passion Window, in the South Aisle, Strasbourg Cathedral, Alsace, France.

This careful depiction is set against decorative blue glass tiles, and with a border of prophets bearing scrolls, foretelling the coming of the King of the Jews. Again, one of the spectators has climbed a nearby tree.

JESUS CLEANSES THE TEMPLE MATTHEW Chapter 21:12–16

AND Jesus went into the temple of God, and cast out all them that sold and bought in the temple, and overthrew the tables of the moneychangers, and the seats of them that sold doves, And said unto them, It is written, My house shall be called the house of prayer; but ye have made it a den of thieves. And the blind and the lame came to him in the temple; and he healed them. And when the chief priests and scribes saw the wonderful things that he did, and the children crying in the temple, and saying, Hosanna to the Son of David; they were sore displeased, And said unto him, Hearest thou what these say? And Jesus saith unto them, Yea; have ye never read, Out of the mouth of babes and sucklings thou hast perfected praise?

The Last Supper
Fifteenth-century window in the Church of St Maria Wiesenkirche, Soest, Westphalia, Germany.

The artist has disregarded Jewish dietary laws by depicting a boar's head being carried to the table. (The Jews were forbidden to eat pork.) Judas is shown with his bag of money in his hand, about to receive the 'sop' from Jesus. The diamond-shaped panes and the heavy heraldic scrollwork are typical of fifteenth-century church glass.

Jesus drives the money-changers from the Temple
Detail from a window by Guillaume de Marcillat, Arezzo Cathedral, Tuscany, Italy; 1519–24.

Notice the attention to detail in this lively scene: the avaricious faces, the panic to shovel loose coins into purses, and the metal scales. The Temple is depicted in Classical style. Very fine leadwork has been used to outline the figures, and only ten narrow iron horizontal bars are used to support the panels, while three larger bars protect the glass from external forces of wind and weather.

MATTHEW
Chapter 26:17–25

The Last Supper
Sixteenth-century window in the Church of St Maria zur Wiese, Soest, Westphalia, Germany.

The artist has disregarded Jewish dietary laws by depicting a boar's head being carried to the table. (The Jews were forbidden to eat pork.) Judas is shown with his bag of money in his hand, about to receive the 'sop' from Jesus. The diamond-shaped panes and the heavy heraldic scrollwork are typical of fifteenth-century church glass.

THE LAST SUPPER

NOW the first day of the feast of unleavened bread the disciples came to Jesus, saying unto him, Where wilt thou that we prepare for thee to eat the passover? And he said, Go into the city to such a man, and say unto him, The Master saith, My time is at hand; I will keep the passover at thy house with my disciples. And the disciples did as Jesus had appointed them; and they made ready the passover. Now when the even was come, he sat down with the twelve. And as they did eat, he said, Verily I say unto you, that one of you shall betray me. And they were exceeding sorrowful, and began every one of them to say unto him, Lord, is it I? And he answered and said, He that dippeth his hand with me in the dish, the same shall betray me. The Son of man goeth as it is written of him: but woe unto that man by whom the Son of man is betrayed! it had been good for that man if he had not been born. Then Judas, which betrayed him, answered and said, Master, is it I? He said unto him, Thou hast said.

The Last Supper
Fourteenth-century window in Freiburg-im-Breisgau Cathedral, Germany.

Judas is tossing the 'sop' of bread into his mouth. In the foreground stands an ornate pewter carafe with a German-style hinged lid.

Christ's agony in the Garden of Gethsemane
A fifteenth-century window by Hans Acker in the Besserer Chapel, Ulm Cathedral, Germany.

This window has emphatically heavy lead outlines, which were not necessary for load-bearing purposes in so small a panel. However, they seem to add to the sombre tone of the picture.

The agony in the garden
A cartoon by Charles Larivière, executed by Béranger, in the Chapelle Royale, Dreux, France; 1845.

JESUS' AGONY IN THE GARDEN — LUKE Chapter 22:39–46

AND he came out, and went, as he was wont, to the mount of Olives; and his disciples also followed him. And when he was at the place, he said unto them, Pray that ye enter not into temptation. And he was withdrawn from them about a stone's cast, and kneeled down, and prayed, Saying, Father, if thou be willing, remove this cup from me: nevertheless not my will, but thine, be done. And there appeared an angel unto him from heaven, strengthening him. And being in an agony he prayed more earnestly: and his sweat was as it were great drops of blood falling down to the ground. And when he rose up from prayer, and was come to his disciples, he found them sleeping for sorrow, And said unto them, Why sleep ye? rise and pray, lest ye enter into temptation.

Christ before Pilate
Fifteenth-century window by Hans Acker in the Besserer Chapel, Ulm Cathedral, Germany.

Peculiar to this depiction is the falcon chained to its perch in Pilate's audience chamber. Jesus wears the dark royal purple robe mockingly put on him by the Roman soldiers. Notice the two little heraldic shields decorated with the Roman eagle. This window was heavily renovated in the nineteenth century.

The betrayal of Christ
A sixteenth-century Flemish panel in Llanwenllwyfo Church, Anglesey, North Wales.

In this dramatic scene, full of heated action, Judas is almost unnoticed as he walks away (*far right-hand side of the picture*). The upper part of the panel has been crudely repaired, with random use of heavy lead.

LUKE
Chapter 22:47–53

JESUS IS BETRAYED

AND while he yet spake, behold a multitude, and he that was called Judas, one of the twelve, went before them, and drew near unto Jesus to kiss him. But Jesus said unto him, Judas, betrayest thou the Son of man with a kiss? When they which were about him saw what would follow, they said unto him, Lord, shall we smite with the sword?

And one of them smote the servant of the high priest, and cut off his right ear. And Jesus answered and said, Suffer ye thus far. And he touched his ear, and healed him. Then Jesus said unto the chief priests, and captains of the temple, and the elders, which were come to him, Be ye come out, as against a thief, with swords and staves? When I was daily with you in the temple, ye stretched forth no hands against me: but this is your hour, and the power of darkness.

Christ before Caiaphas
A fifteenth-century panel from the Rhineland, Germany; now in the St Mary's Church, Stoke D'Abernon, Surrey, England.

The Jewish High Priest Caiaphas is depicted making an imploring gesture (see Matthew 26:63).

Christ before Pilate
A fifteenth-century panel in the Chapel of the Sacrament, Cologne Cathedral, Germany.

The exaggeratedly large faces of the bullying soldiers and peasants stress their cruelty and hatred. Pilate is portrayed in the act of symbolically washing his hands.

MATTHEW
Chapter 27:19–26

JESUS BEFORE PILATE

WHEN he [Pilate] was set down on the judgment seat, his wife sent unto him, saying, Have thou nothing to do with that just man: for I have suffered many things this day in a dream because of him. But the chief priests and elders persuaded the multitude that they should ask Barabbas, and destroy Jesus. The governor answered and said unto them, Whether of the twain will ye that I release unto you? They said, Barabbas. Pilate saith unto them, What shall I do then with Jesus which is called Christ? They all say unto him, Let him be crucified. And the governor said, Why, what evil hath he done? But they cried out the more, saying, Let him be crucified.

When Pilate saw that he could prevail nothing, but that rather a tumult was made, he took water, and washed his hands before the multitude, saying, I am innocent of the blood of this just person: see ye to it. Then answered all the people, and said, His blood be on us, and on our children.

Then released he Barabbas unto them: and when he had scourged Jesus, he delivered him to be crucified.

The mocking of Christ ▷
Panel from the fifteenth-century Passion Window, Church of La Madeleine, Troyes, France.

Jesus is here shown blindfolded, being taunted to name his assailants as they spit at him and strike him.

The scourging of Christ ◁
Fifteenth-century window in the Chapel of the Sacrament, Cologne Cathedral, Germany.

The soldiers hold two instruments of torture: a barbed flail and a scourge of bound canes. The pillar to which Jesus is bound is depicted in royal purple, to signify Jesus' royal title, the King of the Jews. Jesus' hand already has a hole drawn in it, prefiguring the nail-hole of the cross.

JESUS IS SCOURGED AND MOCKED MATTHEW Chapter 27:27–31

THEN the soldiers of the governor took Jesus into the common hall, and gathered unto him the whole band of soldiers. And they stripped him, and put on him a scarlet robe.

And when they had platted a crown of thorns, they put it upon his head, and a reed in his right hand: and they bowed the knee before him, and mocked him, saying, Hail, King of the Jews! And they spit upon him, and took the reed, and smote him on the head. And after that they had mocked him, they took the robe off from him, and put his own raiment on him, and led him away to crucify him.

The mocking of Jesus ▽
Sixteenth-century window in the Church of La Madeleine, Vermeuil, France.

Jesus' robe is here coloured royal blue, instead of the traditional purple. The guards wear identical striped uniforms of jerkin and hose; the man in the foreground is splashed by blood from the crown of thorns being beaten into Jesus' head. The glass for the hand of the kneeling soldier has been damaged. Each soldier's right hand is gloved with a leather mitt, used to handle the thorn bush from which the crown was plaited.

Proph
tiza q te percussit

PETER DENIES CHRIST

AND they led Jesus away to the high priest: and with him were assembled all the chief priests and the elders and the scribes. And Peter followed him afar off, even into the palace of the high priest: and he sat with the servants, and warmed himself at the fire. And the chief priests and all the council sought for witness against Jesus to put him to death; and found none. For many bare false witness against him, but their witness agreed not together. And there arose certain, and bare false witness against him, saying, We heard him say, I will destroy this temple that is made with hands, and within three days I will build another made without hands. But neither so did their witness agree together. And the high priest stood up in the midst, and asked Jesus, saying, Answerest thou nothing? what is it which these witness against thee? But he held his peace, and answered nothing. Again the high priest asked him, and said unto him, Art thou the Christ, the Son of the Blessed? And Jesus said, I am: and ye shall see the Son of man sitting on the right hand of power, and coming in the clouds of heaven. Then the high priest rent his clothes, and saith, What need we any further witnesses? Ye have heard the blasphemy: what think ye? And they all condemned him to be guilty of death. And some began to spit on him, and to cover his face, and to buffet him, and to say unto him, Prophesy: and the servants did strike him with the palms of their hands.

And as Peter was beneath in the palace, there cometh one of the maids of the high priest: And when she saw Peter warming himself, she looked upon him, and said, And thou also wast with Jesus of Nazareth. But he denied, saying, I know not, neither understand I what thou sayest. And he went out into the porch; and the cock crew. And a maid saw him again, and began to say to them that stood by, This is one of them. And he denied it again. And a little after, they that stood by said again to Peter, Surely thou art one of them: for thou art a Galilaean, and thy speech agreeth thereto. But he began to curse and to swear, saying, I know not this man of whom ye speak. And the second time the cock crew. And Peter called to mind the word that Jesus said unto him, Before the cock crow twice, thou shalt deny me thrice. And when he thought thereon, he wept.

MARK
Chapter 14:53–72

Peter's denial
Detail from Lancet B in the twentieth-century Prisoners of Conscience Window by Gabriel Loire, Salisbury Cathedral, Wiltshire, England.

The cockerel is depicted partly in red, partly in brilliant blue, often known as 'Chartres blue'. This is not surprising, for the artist, Gabriel Loire, works from an atelier in Lêves, near Chartres, and has introduced this characteristic colour into windows as far apart as Japan, Mexico and Africa as well as in Western Europe.

Peter's denial
Twentieth-century window by Hans Gottfried von Stockhausen in the Besserer Chapel, Ulm Cathedral, Germany.

How much emotional force is conveyed by the faces in this window: the smug maidservant; Peter, lit by the fire, as if burning in the private hell of his own sad thoughts; the curious hangers-on.

ON THE WAY TO THE CROSS

AND as they led him away, they laid hold upon one Simon, a Cyrenian, coming out of the country, and on him they laid the cross, that he might bear it after Jesus.

And there followed him a great company of people, and of women, which also bewailed and lamented him. But Jesus turning unto them said, Daughters of Jerusalem, weep not for me, but weep for yourselves, and for your children. For, behold, the days are coming, in the which they shall say, Blessed are the barren, and the wombs that never bare, and the paps which never gave suck. Then shall they begin to say to the mountains, Fall on us; and to the hills, Cover us. For if they do these things in a green tree, what shall be done in the dry?

LUKE
Chapter 23:26–31

Simon of Cyrene
From St John's Church, Gouda, Holland; 1559.

This window offers splendidly detailed illustrations of contemporary Dutch clothing. The two criminals who were crucified with Jesus are here portrayed as young men.

Christ carrying the cross
Twentieth-century window by Gabriel Loire, Coignières Church, near Versailles, northern France.

The imprint of Jesus' face is seen on the kerchief of the traditional figure of Veronica, who is supposed to have used the cloth to wipe the blood and sweat from his face as he carried the cross to Golgotha.

Casting dice for Christ's robe
Detail from a fifteenth-century window in the Chapel of the Holy Sacrament, Cologne Cathedral, Germany.

A rare subject in stained glass, with small details underlining that, for the soldiers, a crucifixion was part of their daily experience. Other perceptive details in this busy scene include an auger used to bore holes for the nails; a soldier wielding the flail, and the hooded figure bearing the inscription placed over the crucified Jesus.

MATTHEW
Chapter 27:33–44

AND when they were come unto a place called Golgotha, that is to say, a place of a skull,

They gave him vinegar to drink mingled with gall: and when he had tasted thereof, he would not drink. And they crucified him, and parted his garments, casting lots: that it might be fulfilled which was spoken by the prophet, They parted my garments among them, and upon my vesture did they cast lots. And sitting down they watched him there; And set up over his head his accusation written, THIS IS JESUS THE KING OF THE JEWS. Then were there two thieves crucified with him, one on the right hand, and another on the left.

And they that passed by reviled him, wagging their heads, And saying, Thou that destroyest the temple, and buildest it in three days, save thyself. If thou be the Son of God, come down from the cross. Likewise also the chief priests mocking him, with the scribes and elders, said, He saved others; himself he cannot save. If he be the King of Israel, let him now come down from the cross, and we will believe him. He trusted in God; let him deliver him now, if he will have him: for he said, I am the Son of God. The thieves also, which were crucified with him, cast the same in his teeth.

The Crucifixion
Fourteenth-century window in the Kloster Kirche, Königsfelden, Switzerland.

This window consists of three roundels, the lowest showing the flagellation of Christ. Jesus is tied to a pillar, purple to signify his royal lineage, which is further emphasized by the Lion of Judah – emblem of the line of David – at the base of each roundel. The central roundel presents the significant figures in a crucifixion scene of poignant simplicity. Mary, mother of Jesus (*left*) is comforted by another woman; Mary Magdalene, bare-headed to denote her inferior status, carries a box of embalming oils. The soldier behind her holds the wine-vinegar which was offered to the dying Jesus. The top roundel shows the taking down of Jesus' body from the cross. The workmen's heads are exaggeratedly large, so that they may be seen clearly from below. The workmen carry the tools of their trade, including a claw-hammer in the belt.

Christ is nailed to the cross
Window from the Rhineland, near Cologne, Germany; now in St Mary's Church, Stoke D'Abernon, Surrey, England.

To draw attention to his theme, the artist has exaggerated the size of the nails. Two men strain on ropes round Christ's wrist to stretch the arm that will bear the body's weight.

THE CRUCIFIXION

Now from the sixth hour there was darkness over all the land unto the ninth hour. And about the ninth hour Jesus cried with a loud voice, saying, Eli, Eli, lama sabachthani? that is to say, My God, my God, why hast thou forsaken me? Some of them that stood there, when they heard that, said, This man calleth for Elias. And straightway one of them ran, and took a spunge, and filled it with vinegar, and put it on a reed, and gave him to drink. The rest said, Let be, let us see whether Elias will come to save him.

Jesus, when he had cried again with a loud voice, yielded up the ghost. And, behold, the veil of the temple was rent in twain from the top to the bottom; and the earth did quake, and the rocks rent; And the graves were opened; and many bodies of the saints which slept arose, And came out of the graves after his resurrection, and went into the holy city, and appeared unto many. Now when the centurion, and they that were with him, watching Jesus, saw the earthquake, and those things that were done, they feared greatly, saying, Truly this was the Son of God. And many women were there beholding afar off, which followed Jesus from Galilee, ministering unto him: Among which was Mary Magdalene, and Mary the mother of James and Joses, and the mother of Zebedee's children.

MATTHEW
Chapter 27:45–56

The Crucifixion
Fourteenth-century window in the Church of St Michael and All Angels, Eaton Bishop, Herefordshire, England.

The cross is here shown as made of green wood, to signify new life springing from death. Mary's fingers are interlaced, to reflect her own agony. The small book in John's hand represents his Gospel. The panel is framed by entwined vines, perhaps reflecting Jesus' claim to be the True Vine.

The Crucifixion
A fourteenth-century Flemish window in Llanwenllwyfo Church, Anglesey, North Wales.

The partially-eclipsed moon perhaps indicates the great darkness that followed Christ's death. While the two thieves are roped to their crosses, Jesus is nailed to his. The skull and thighbone are possibly intended to reflect the name of the execution site, 'the place of the skull' – Golgotha.

THE Jews therefore, because it was the preparation, that the bodies should not remain upon the cross on the sabbath day, (for that sabbath day was an high day,) besought Pilate that their legs might be broken, and that they might be taken away. Then came the soldiers, and brake the legs of the first, and of the other which was crucified with him. But when they came to Jesus, and saw that he was dead already, they brake not his legs: But one of the soldiers with a spear pierced his side, and forthwith came there out blood and water. And he that saw it bare record, and his record is true: and he knoweth that he saith true, that ye might believe. For these things were done, that the scripture should be fulfilled, A bone of him shall not be broken. And again another scripture saith, They shall look on him whom they pierced.

JOHN
Chapter 19:31–42

The deposition from the cross
Window by Andrea del Castagno, Florence Cathedral, Italy; 1444.

Sometimes known as the *Pieta*, the roundel shows in terrible detail the tortured, broken body of Christ. Mary's normally gentle face is contorted by grief. Mary Magdalene, in bright, gaudy robes, offers embalming ointments. Only the base of the cross is shown; the artist could concentrate on facial expressions instead of illustrating the familiar scene in its entirety once again.

And after this Joseph of Arimathaea, being a disciple of Jesus, but secretly for fear of the Jews, besought Pilate that he might take away the body of Jesus: and Pilate gave him leave. He came therefore, and took the body of Jesus. And there came also Nicodemus, which at the first came to Jesus by night, and brought a mixture of myrrh and aloes, about an hundred pound weight. Then took they the body of Jesus, and wound it in linen clothes with the spices, as the manner of the Jews is to bury. Now in the place where he was crucified there was a garden; and in the garden a new sepulchre, wherein was never man yet laid. There laid they Jesus therefore because of the Jews' preparation day; for the sepulchre was nigh at hand.

The Entombment
Twelfth-century window at Rivenhall Church, Essex, England.

A roundel of exquisite simplicity which reflects the pathos of carrying the body of Christ in its long winding-sheet to the empty tomb. Light comes from the elongated flame of a single oil-lamp.

THE RESURRECTION

AND when the sabbath was past, Mary Magdalene, and Mary the mother of James, and Salome, had bought sweet spices, that they might come and anoint him. And very early in the morning the first day of the week, they came unto the sepulchre at the rising of the sun. And they said among themselves, Who shall roll us away the stone from the door of the sepulchre? And when they looked, they saw that the stone was rolled away: for it was very great. And entering into the sepulchre, they saw a young man sitting on the right side, clothed in a long white garment; and they were affrighted. And he saith unto them, Be not affrighted: Ye seek Jesus of Nazareth, which was crucified: he is risen; he is not here: behold the place where they laid him. But go your way, tell his disciples and Peter that he goeth before you into Galilee: there shall ye see him, as he said unto you. And they went out quickly, and fled from the sepulchre; for they trembled and were amazed: neither said they any thing to any man; for they were afraid.

MARK
Chapter 16:1–8

The three women go to the tomb
Detail from the fifteenth-century Passion Window, La Madeleine, Troyes, France.

Mary, the mother of Christ, Mary Magdalene, and Mary mother of James come to the tomb bearing jars of embalming ointment. Three matchstick soldiers are depicted very small in the background. Three symbolic fruit hang from the tree.

The Resurrection
Fourteenth-century window in the Kloster Kirche, Königsfelden, Switzerland.

Three lights, each portraying individual scenes, are backed by blue glass 'tiles' typical of this period. The sleeping guards wear full chain-mail; both sun and moon watch the resurrection.

MAGD

JOHN
Chapter 20:24–29

Mary Magdalene meets Jesus in the garden
Sixteenth-century Flemish panel, now in Llanwenllwyfo Church, Anglesey, North Wales.

The artist has depicted Mary Magdalene robed in the height of sixteenth century fashion; her hair in a snood, her name embroidered on 'cuffs' below the shoulder. In contrast, Christ, who was mistaken by Mary for the gardener, is barefoot and wears a peasant's straw hat. Contemporary Flemish rural life is reflected in the farmhouse, barns and cart.

Doubting Thomas
Sixteenth-century window in the Church of St Mary, Fairford, Gloucestershire, England.

This panel has been severely damaged by weathering and atmospheric pollution. Pitting and pock-marking, clearly visible on Christ's face and hands, has been caused by polluted rain. In addition, Thomas's red robe-sleeves are stained, and the glass has cracked and been repaired with a spider's web of lead. Fortunately Thomas's probing fingers, the main witness of his doubt, are undamaged.

DOUBTING THOMAS

But Thomas, one of the twelve, called Didymus, was not with them when Jesus came. The other disciples therefore said unto him, We have seen the Lord. But he said unto them, Except I shall see in his hands the print of the nails, and put my finger into the print of the nails, and thrust my hand into his side, I will not believe.

And after eight days again his disciples were within, and Thomas with them: then came Jesus, the doors being shut, and stood in the midst, and said, Peace be unto you. Then saith he to Thomas, Reach hither thy finger, and behold my hands; and reach hither thy hand, and thrust it into my side: and be not faithless, but believing. And Thomas answered and said unto him, My Lord and my God. Jesus saith unto him, Thomas, because thou hast seen me, thou hast believed: blessed are they that have not seen, and yet have believed.

The road to Emmaus
A seventeenth-century Swiss panel, now in the Darmstadt Museum, Germany.

This window is made of painted glass; the trees of the mountain landscape depicted in a variety of greens and blues. The two travellers wear broad-brimmed hats, leather boots and jackets over short kilts; the stranger is robed in blue.

ON THE WAY TO EMMAUS

LUKE
Chapter 24:13–32

AND, behold, two of them went that same day to a village called Emmaus, which was from Jerusalem about threescore furlongs. And they talked together of all these things which had happened. And it came to pass, that, while they communed together and reasoned, Jesus himself drew near, and went with them. But their eyes were holden that they should not know him. And he said unto them, What manner of communications are these that ye have one to another, as ye walk, and are sad? And the one of them, whose name was Cleopas, answering said unto him, Art thou only a stranger in Jerusalem, and hast not known the things which are come to pass there in these days? And he said unto them, What things? And they said unto him, Concerning Jesus of Nazareth, which was a prophet mighty in deed and word before God and all the people: And how the chief priests and our rulers delivered him to be condemned to death, and have crucified him. But we trusted that it had been he which should have redeemed Israel: and beside all this, to day is the third day since these things were done. Yea, and certain women also of our company made us astonished, which were early at the sepulchre; And when they found not his body, they came, saying, that they had also seen a vision of angels, which said that he was alive. And certain of them which were with us went to the sepulchre, and found it even so as the women had said: but him they saw not. Then he said unto them, O fools, and slow of heart to believe all that the prophets have spoken: Ought not Christ to have suffered these things, and to enter into his glory? And beginning at Moses and all the prophets, he expounded unto them in all the scriptures the things concerning himself. And they drew nigh unto the village, whither they went: and he made as though he would have gone further. But they constrained him, saying, Abide with us: for it is toward evening, and the day is far spent. And he went in to tarry with them. And it came to pass, as he sat at meat with them, he took bread, and blessed it, and brake, and gave to them. And their eyes were opened, and they knew him; and he vanished out of their sight. And they said one to another, Did not our heart burn within us, while he talked with us by the way, and while he opened to us the scriptures?

The supper at Emmaus
Panel from a sixteenth-century window in the Church of St Pierre, Dreux, France.

The disciples show astonished recognition as Christ blesses the cottage loaf before eating. James, with his emblem of a shell on his hat, shows chagrin on recognizing Christ. Jesus grasps the spiked staff of a traveller.

JESUS APPEARS BY THE SEA

AFTER these things Jesus shewed himself again to the disciples at the sea of Tiberias; and on this wise shewed he himself. There were together Simon Peter, and Thomas called Didymus, and Nathanael of Cana in Galilee, and the sons of Zebedee, and two other of his disciples. Simon Peter saith unto them, I go a fishing. They say unto him, We also go with thee. They went forth, and entered into a ship immediately; and that night they caught nothing. But when the morning was now come, Jesus stood on the shore: but the disciples knew not that it was Jesus. Then Jesus saith unto them, Children, have ye any meat? They answered him, No. And he said unto them, Cast the net on the right side of the ship, and ye shall find. They cast therefore, and now they were not able to draw it for the multitude of fishes. Therefore that disciple whom Jesus loved saith unto Peter, It is the Lord. Now when Simon Peter heard that it was the Lord, he girt his fisher's coat unto him, (for he was naked,) and did cast himself into the sea. And the other disciples came in a little ship; (for they were not far from land, but as it were two hundred cubits,) dragging the net with fishes. As soon then as they were come to land, they saw a fire of coals there, and fish laid thereon, and bread. Jesus saith unto them, Bring of the fish which ye

JOHN
Chapter 21:1–14

The miraculous draught of fish
A twentieth-century sexfoil window by Wailles, Bradfield College, Berkshire, England.

The artist has ingeniously included all the main elements of the story in this unusual design. The heavy draught of fishes includes a conger eel. Christ has already lit the fire to cook breakfast.

have now caught. Simon Peter went up, and drew the net to land full of great fishes, an hundred and fifty and three: and for all there were so many, yet was not the net broken. Jesus saith unto them, Come and dine. And none of the disciples durst ask him, Who art thou? knowing that it was the Lord. Jesus then cometh, and taketh bread, and giveth them, and fish likewise. This is now the third time that Jesus shewed himself to his disciples, after that he was risen from the dead.

Breakfast on the Sea of Galilee
Three lights from a twentieth-century window, St George's Church, Georgeham, North Devon, England.

The three lights together form the entire scene. Although the men are 'frozen' in time, there is a strong feeling of action, focussed on the figure of Jesus in the golden robe. The faces are timeless, and although the figures are dressed in biblical clothes, the essential feeling is modern.

Christ's charge to Peter
Panel by Gabriel Loire in Coignières Church, near Paris, France; 1975.

Two huge keys draw attention to the theme of this window – Christ's commission to Peter. The dimly-seen buildings probably represent Rome. The fine mesh texture across Peter's arms is very characteristic of Loire's work. Christ looks directly at Peter, whose bowed head reflects his agony as he recalls his denials of his master.

JOHN
Chapter 21:15–25

JESUS' CHARGE TO PETER

SO when they had dined, Jesus saith to Simon Peter, Simon, son of Jonas, lovest thou me more than these? He saith unto him, Yea, Lord; thou knowest that I love thee. He saith unto him, Feed my lambs. He saith to him again the second time, Simon, son of Jonas, lovest thou me? He saith unto him, Yea, Lord; thou knowest that I love thee. He saith unto him, Feed my sheep. He saith unto him the third time, Simon, son of Jonas, lovest thou me? Peter was grieved because he said unto him the third time, Lovest thou me? And he said unto him, Lord, thou knowest all things; thou knowest that I love thee. Jesus saith unto him, Feed my sheep. Verily, verily, I say unto thee, When thou wast young, thou girdedst thyself, and walkedst whither thou wouldest: but when thou shalt be old, thou shalt stretch forth thy hands, and another shall gird thee, and carry thee whither thou wouldest not. This spake he, signifying by what death he should glorify God. And when he had spoken this, he saith unto him, Follow me.

Then Peter, turning about, seeth the disciple whom Jesus loved following; which also leaned on his breast at supper, and said, Lord, which is he that betrayeth thee? Peter seeing him saith to Jesus, Lord, and what shall this man do? Jesus saith unto him, If I will that he tarry till I come, what is that to thee? follow thou me. Then went this saying abroad among the brethren, that that disciple should not die: yet Jesus said not unto him, He shall not die; but, If I will that he tarry till I come, what is that to thee? This is the disciple which testifieth of these things, and wrote these things: and we know that his testimony is true. And there are also many other things which Jesus did, the which, if they should be written every one, I suppose that even the world itself could not contain the books that should be written. Amen.

Christ's charge to Peter
Nineteenth-century window, after Raphael's drawing, in the South Nave, St Chad's Church, Prees, Shropshire, England.

Christ's finger points to the keys, which Peter holds close to his heart. The sub-title of the window is 'Feed my sheep', and symbolic sheep are also depicted.

The Ascension
Fourteenth-century panel from the Tulenhaupt Window, in the South Aisle, Freiburg-im-Breisgau Cathedral, Germany.

An extremely stylized rendering of this subject. Christ is shown making the sign of blessing; the angels wait to lift his throne. The green mound represents the world which Christ is leaving.

THE ASCENSION

ACTS
Chapter 1:1–14

THE former treatise have I made, O Theophilus, of all that Jesus began both to do and teach, Until the day in which he was taken up, after that he through the Holy Ghost had given commandments unto the apostles whom he had chosen: To whom also he shewed himself alive after his passion by many infallible proofs, being seen of them forty days, and speaking of the things pertaining to the kingdom of God: And, being assembled together with them, commanded them that they should not depart from Jerusalem, but wait for the promise of the Father, which, saith he, ye have heard of me. For John truly baptized with water; but ye shall be baptized with the Holy Ghost not many days hence. When they therefore were come together, they asked of him, saying, Lord, wilt thou at this time restore again the kingdom to Israel? And he said unto them, It is not for you to know the times or the seasons, which the Father hath put in his own power. But ye shall receive power, after that the Holy Ghost is come upon you: and ye shall be witnesses unto me both in Jerusalem, and in all Judaea, and in Samaria, and unto the uttermost part of the earth. And when he had spoken these things, while they beheld, he was taken up; and a cloud received him out of their sight. And while they looked stedfastly toward heaven as he went up, behold, two men stood by them in white apparel;

Which also said, Ye men of Galilee, why stand ye gazing up into heaven? this same Jesus, which is taken up from you into heaven, shall so come in like manner as ye have seen him go into heaven. Then returned they unto Jerusalem from the mount called Olivet, which is from Jerusalem a sabbath day's journey. And when they were come in, they went up into an upper room, where abode both Peter, and James, and John, and Andrew, Philip, and Thomas, Bartholomew, and Matthew, James the son of Alphaeus, and Simon Zelotes, and Judas the brother of James. These all continued with one accord in prayer and supplication, with the women, and Mary the mother of Jesus, and with his brethren.

The Ascension
Three panels from a twelfth-century window in Le Mans Cathedral, France.

Close observation shows that this window has been patched clumsily with glass fragments which were to hand; for example tiny claw-like hands are used to represent feet. The willowy curves of the human figures are characteristic of this early date.

PENTECOST

AND when the day of Pentecost was fully come, they were all with one accord in one place. And suddenly there came a sound from heaven as of a rushing mighty wind, and it filled all the house where they were sitting. And there appeared unto them cloven tongues like as of fire, and it sat upon each of them. And they were all filled with the Holy Ghost, and began to speak with other tongues, as the Spirit gave them utterance. And there were dwelling at Jerusalem Jews, devout men, out of every nation under heaven. Now when this was noised abroad, the multitude came together, and were confounded, because that every man heard them speak in his own language. And they were all amazed and marvelled, saying one to another, Behold, are not all these which speak Galilaeans? And how hear we every man in our own tongue, wherein we were born? Parthians, and Medes, and Elamites, and the dwellers in Mesopotamia, and in Judaea, and Cappadocia, in Pontus, and Asia, Phrygia, and Pamphylia, in Egypt, and in the parts of Libya about Cyrene, and strangers of Rome, Jews and proselytes, Cretes and Arabians, we do hear them speak in our tongues the wonderful works of God. And they were all amazed, and were in doubt, saying one to another, What meaneth this? Others mocking said, These men are full of new wine.

But Peter, standing up with the eleven, lifted up his voice, and said unto them, Ye men of Judaea, and all ye that dwell at Jerusalem, be this known unto you, and hearken to my words: For these are not drunken, as ye suppose, seeing it is but the third hour of the day. But this is that which was spoken by the prophet Joel; And it shall come to pass in the last days, saith God, I will pour out of my Spirit upon all flesh: and your sons and your daughters shall prophesy, and your young men shall see visions, and your old men shall dream dreams: And on my servants and on my handmaidens I will pour out in those days of my Spirit; and they shall prophesy: And I will shew wonders in heaven above, and signs in the earth beneath; blood, and fire, and vapour of smoke: The sun shall be turned into darkness, and the moon into blood, before that great and notable day of the Lord come: And it shall come to pass, that whosoever shall call on the name of the Lord shall be saved. Ye men of Israel, hear these words; Jesus of Nazareth, a man approved of God among you by miracles and wonders and signs, which God did by him in the midst of you, as ye yourselves also know: Him, being delivered by the determinate counsel and foreknowledge of God, ye have taken, and by wicked hands have crucified and slain: Whom God hath raised up, having loosed the pains of death: because it was not possible that he should be holden of it.

ACTS
Chapter 2:1–24

Pentecost
Window in the chapel of St John's Church, Gouda, Holland; 1556.

The barely-discernible tongues of fire descending on the apostles appear almost like little feathers on their heads. The Holy Spirit is depicted as a dove.

Pentecost
Panel from a fifteenth-century window in the Besserer Chapel, Ulm Cathedral, Germany.

The tongues of fire are difficult to discern amongst the apostles' curly hair; the sign is more clearly visible within the halo surrounding Mary's head. Tongues of fire are also seen emanating from the book representing the New Testament, signifying its inspiration.

PETER AND JOHN HEAL A LAME MAN

Now Peter and John went up together into the temple at the hour of prayer, being the ninth hour. And a certain man lame from his mother's womb was carried, whom they laid daily at the gate of the temple which is called Beautiful, to ask alms of them that entered into the temple; Who seeing Peter and John about to go into the temple asked an alms. And Peter, fastening his eyes upon him with John, said, Look on us. And he gave heed unto them, expecting to receive something of them. Then Peter said, Silver and gold have I none; but such as I have give I thee: In the name of Jesus Christ of Nazareth rise up and walk. And he took him by the right hand, and lifted him up: and immediately his feet and ancle bones received strength. And he leaping up stood, and walked, and entered with them into the temple, walking, and leaping, and praising God. And all the people saw him walking and praising God: And they knew that it was he which sat for alms at the Beautiful gate of the temple: and they were filled with wonder and amazement at that which had happened unto him. And as the lame man which was healed held Peter and John, all the people ran together unto them in the porch that is called Solomon's, greatly wondering.

And when Peter saw it, he answered unto the people, Ye men of Israel, why marvel ye at this? or why look ye so earnestly on us, as though by our own power or holiness we had made this man to walk? The God of Abraham, and of Isaac, and of Jacob, the God of our fathers, hath glorified his Son Jesus; whom ye delivered up, and denied him in the presence of Pilate, when he was determined to let him go. But ye denied the Holy One and the Just, and desired a murderer to be granted unto you; And killed the Prince of life, whom God hath raised from the dead; whereof we are witnesses. And his name through faith in his name hath made this man strong, whom ye see and know: yea, the faith which is by him hath given him this perfect soundness in the presence of you all. And now, brethren, I wot that through ignorance ye did it, as did also your rulers. But those things, which God before had shewed by the mouth of all his prophets, that Christ should suffer, he hath so fulfilled.

ACTS
Chapter 3:1–18

Peter heals a cripple at the Gate Beautiful
Window by Joshua Price in Great Witley Church, Worcestershire, England; 1719.

This window is extremely rare in having its date and the name of its creator clearly engraved. The beggar is seated on a low wooden-wheeled platform with a rag-bound handle; Peter bears a symbolic key. The large white rose high up on a pillar is the mark of the Lancashire glaziers.

:Price 1719

PETER IN PRISON

ACTS
Chapter 12:1–5

Now about that time Herod the king stretched forth his hands to vex certain of the church. And he killed James the brother of John with the sword. And because he saw it pleased the Jews, he proceeded further to take Peter also. (Then were the days of unleavened bread.) And when he had apprehended him, he put him in prison, and delivered him to four quaternions of soldiers to keep him; intending after Easter to bring him forth to the people. Peter therefore was kept in prison: but prayer was made without ceasing of the church unto God for him.

The conversion of Paul
Panel from a nineteenth-century window, Lincoln Cathedral, England.

Paul is shown already haloed, though this window shows his conversion. The glass has been chosen for its strong, deep colours. The main figures in this panel are made from large sections of glass; bars hold the whole panel in place.

Peter in prison
Panel from a nineteenth-century window in Lincoln Cathedral, England.

This panel is clearly and incisively drawn, and brilliantly coloured.

ACTS
Chapter 9:1–8

Paul escapes from Damascus
Window 6, the Chapter House, York Minster, England; fourteenth century.

Paul is lowered in a basket from the walls of Damascus. To stress Paul's importance, the artist has drawn his balding head larger than the soldiers behind the wall (*right*). In a window composed of so many small, heavily-leaded pieces, it is at first difficult to distinguish the scene.

SAUL'S CONVERSION

AND Saul, yet breathing out threatenings and slaughter against the disciples of the Lord, went unto the high priest, And desired of him letters to Damascus to the synagogues, that if he found any of this way, whether they were men or women, he might bring them bound unto Jerusalem. And as he journeyed, he came near Damascus: and suddenly there shined round about him a light from heaven: And he fell to the earth, and heard a voice saying unto him, Saul, Saul, why persecutest thou me? And he said, Who art thou, Lord? And the Lord said, I am Jesus whom thou persecutest: it is hard for thee to kick against the pricks. And he trembling and astonished said, Lord, what wilt thou have me to do? And the Lord said unto him, Arise, and go into the city, and it shall be told thee what thou must do. And the men which journeyed with him stood speechless, hearing a voice, but seeing no man. And Saul arose from the earth; and when his eyes were opened, he saw no man: but they led him by the hand, and brought him into Damascus.

PAUL IN PRISON

AND it came to pass, as we went to prayer, a certain damsel possessed with a spirit of divination met us, which brought her masters much gain by soothsaying: The same followed Paul and us, and cried, saying, These men are the servants of the most high God, which shew unto us the way of salvation. And this did she many days. But Paul, being grieved, turned and said to the spirit, I command thee in the name of Jesus Christ to come out of her. And he came out the same hour.

And when her masters saw that the hope of their gains was gone, they caught Paul and Silas, and drew them into the marketplace unto the rulers, And brought them to the magistrates, saying, These men, being Jews, do exceedingly trouble our city, And teach customs, which are not lawful for us to receive, neither to observe, being Romans. And the multitude rose up together against them: and the magistrates rent off their clothes, and commanded to beat them. And when they had laid many stripes upon them, they cast them into prison, charging the jailor to keep them safely: Who, having received such a charge, thrust them into the inner prison, and made their feet fast in the stocks.

And at midnight Paul and Silas prayed, and sang praises unto God: and the prisoners heard them. And suddenly there was a great earthquake, so that the foundations of the prison were shaken: and immediately all the doors were opened, and every one's bands were loosed.

ACTS
Chapter 16: 16–26

The Apostle Paul
Detail from the great fifteenth-century West Window, Canterbury Cathedral, Kent, England.

Paul is shown holding a book – signifying his epistles – and a sword, his emblem, symbolizing the sword of the Spirit (Ephesians 6:17).

Paul in prison
Seventeenth-century Flemish panel, now in St Mary Magdalene, Mulbarton, Norfolk, England.

The heavily-shackled prisoners are grouped together. Two small roundels depict food and drink. This probably represents Paul and Timothy in prison, visited by Epaphroditus (*centre*), with his donation from Philippi (Philippians 4).

REVELATION
Chapter 6:1–8

The Four Horsemen of the Apocalypse
Panel 9 in the Apocalypse Window, Church of St Florentin, France; 1529.

Men and women are ridden down; warhorses with staring eyes charge; terrified people vainly make the two-fingered anti-Satanic sign against the evil eye. This window is secured rigidly by thick iron bars.

The Last Judgement
Panel from a thirteenth-century window, Bourges Cathedral, France.

The vast dragon represents Hell; the devils rake and push wrongdoers into the flames belching from its gaping jaws.

THE APOCALYPSE

AND I saw when the Lamb opened one of the seals, and I heard, as it were the noise of thunder, one of the four beasts saying, Come and see. And I saw, and behold a white horse: and he that sat on him had a bow; and a crown was given unto him: and he went forth conquering, and to conquer. And when he had opened the second seal, I heard the second beast say, Come and see. And there went out another horse that was red: and power was given to him that sat thereon to take peace from the earth, and that they should kill one another: and there was given unto him a great sword. And when he had opened the third seal, I heard the third beast say, Come and see. And I beheld, and lo a black horse; and he that sat on him had a pair of balances in his hand. And I heard a voice in the midst of the four beasts say, A measure of wheat for a penny, and three measures of barley for a penny; and see thou hurt not the oil and the wine. And when he had opened the fourth seal, I heard the voice of the fourth beast say, Come and see. And I looked, and behold a pale horse: and his name that sat on him was Death, and Hell followed with him. And power was given unto them over the fourth part of the earth, to kill with sword, and with hunger, and with death, and with the beasts of the earth.

A NEW HEAVEN AND A NEW EARTH

AND I saw a new heaven and a new earth: for the first heaven and the first earth were passed away; and there was no more sea. And I John saw the holy city, new Jerusalem, coming down from God out of heaven, prepared as a bride adorned for her husband. And I heard a great voice out of heaven saying, Behold, the tabernacle of God is with men, and he will dwell with them, and they shall be his people, and God himself shall be with them, and be their God. And God shall wipe away all tears from their eyes; and there shall be no more death, neither sorrow, nor crying, neither shall there be any more pain: for the former things are passed away. And he that sat upon the throne said, Behold, I make all things new. And he said unto me, Write: for these words are true and faithful. And he said unto me, It is done. I am Alpha and Omega, the beginning and the end. I will give unto him that is athirst of the fountain of the water of life freely. He that overcometh shall inherit all things; and I will be his God, and he shall be my son. But the fearful, and unbelieving, and the abominable, and murderers, and whoremongers, and sorcerers, and idolaters, and all liars, shall have their part in the lake which burneth with fire and brimstone: which is the second death.

REVELATION
Chapter 21:1–8

The Last Judgement
From the sixteenth-century West Window, Fairford Church, Gloucestershire, England.

Christ is seated in majesty on a throne formed from a rainbow, surrounded by apostles, angels and martyrs.

The Last Judgement
Detail from the sixteenth-century Last Judgement Window, Fairford Church, Gloucestershire, England.

At first sight a confusion of scattered red glass, closer inspection of this scene reveals the celebrated 'red devil' coiled about by snakes, the terrified faces and beseeching hands of the damned, and the red-hot instruments of torture. The artist set out to terrify his audience with the torments of damnation.

The Churches

Canterbury Cathedral from the south-west.

In this book we have attempted to illustrate a representative selection of the stained glass of Western Europe, drawing from as wide a variety as possible of periods, styles, countries and artists. But the observant reader will have noticed that a number of medieval cathedrals have been illustrated several times. This is because such cathedrals as Chartres in France, Canterbury in England, and Ulm in Germany contain matchless examples of the glazier's art, and thus demand fuller illustration.

In this brief afterword, we look in a little more detail at the history and nature of the glass in some of these exceptional churches.

Chartres Cathedral

First in any discussion of outstanding stained glass must come the amazing cathedral of Chartres in the Ile de France. Famous throughout the world for its architecture and mystery, Chartres Cathedral boasts some of the most colourful, extensive, and intricate stained glass.

The present church, rebuilt after a disastrous fire in 1194, is at least the sixth church to be built on this historic hill-site. The magnificent building, itself a highpoint of medieval architecture, was finally dedicated in 1260, while most of the stained glass was created between 1215 and 1240. The sheer area available to be glazed was astounding; there are in all 176 windows at Chartres, amounting to a total of some twenty-two thousand square feet of stained glass.

The overall impact of the Chartres glass is achieved by the ever-changing interplay of colour and light. The interior of the cathedral is suffused with subtle variations of colour as the natural light penetrates the deeply stained windows. Even in dull weather the windows have a quality of their own; but in brilliant sunshine some of the dramatic biblical figures depicted in the glass almost seem to spring into life.

Donors

Such a vast series of windows could only have been afforded with generous donations from a large number of people. About four thousand such donors are commemorated in figurative medallions within the windows of Chartres. They include members of the royal family, aristocrats, ecclesiastical leaders, merchants, craftspeople – a cross-section of medieval society, only excepting the forgotten peasantry.

The Norman nave of Great Malvern Priory, Worcestershire, England.

The Ambulatory, Chartres Cathedral, France.

In addition to the windows endowed by these individual benefactors, many of the windows of Chartres were donated by some seventy trade guilds active in the town in the Middle Ages. A total of forty-two windows in the aisles and ambulatory of the cathedral were given by the town guilds of Chartres. The guilds, too, are illustrated in small panels which commemorate their help in embellishing the cathedral.

Often the subject matter of a window is relevant to the trade of the guild responsible; for instance the Noah window, which illustrates the construction of the great Ark, was given by the carpenters, coopers (barrel-makers) and wheelwrights, all of whose work is illustrated in small commemorative panels. Similarly, two bakers with fresh bread are illustrated on the panel showing Moses and the burning bush; and the winemakers' window depicts the use of wine at the mass.

The sixty-four lancet and eye windows of Chartres Cathedral's lower storey, aisles and ambulatory were used to illustrate Bible stories and the lives of the saints, and were intended to educate those worshipping in the church. Placed at a level where they could be read, these windows were indeed the 'Poor Man's Bible', enabling the illiterate to follow and understand important Bible narratives, such as the Good Samaritan or the Annunciation.

The windows of Chartres are a study in themself. Suffice it to say that the visitor is left with a sense of awe at the scope, colour and atmosphere of this supreme example of medieval art, craftsmanship and piety.

Canterbury Cathedral

Like Chartres, Canterbury has a long and auspicious history, and to match it a collection of stained glass of outstanding quality. There has been much discussion about the origins of the Canterbury glass; but, whatever else is in doubt, the quality of the craftsmanship is never in question.

The present cathedral at Canterbury was completed in 1184, having been rebuilt after a disastrous fire in 1174, first by William of Sens, then by William the Englishman. The earliest surviving glass at Canterbury is to be found in the North Rose Window and probably dates from 1178. This great window features various biblical subjects, including Moses with the tablets containing the Ten Commandments, and portraits of the four major prophets, Isaiah, Jeremiah, Ezekiel and Daniel. This is the sole remaining twelfth-century rose window in England.

A series of windows around the choir clerestory originally featured eighty-four figures, representing the ancestors of Christ. Only nine of these windows remain, but they too are striking in the vigour of their artistry.

Ulm Minster

Ulm Minster, in southern Germany, is perhaps supremely a monument to medieval civic pride. It was started in 1377, and became the work of a number of master masons, including Heinrich Parler, Ulrich von Ensingen, who was responsible for the massive west tower, and Matthäus Böblinger.

To match its architectural glories, the cathedral also boasts riches in stained glass. The windows include a fine Jesse Tree, featuring twelve prophets and kings, by the great and prolific fifteenth-century German craftsman Peter Hemmel von Andlau, whose windows are noted for their naturalism and their brilliant reds and blues.

Ulm Minster is also indebted to the Acker family, several generations of whom created fine windows for the cathedral. The oldest windows in the minster, two windows in the choir depicting the life of Mary and her legendary mother, Anne, are believed to be by the Acker family. But probably the most outstanding windows from this family are by Hans Acker, who was employed by the wealthy Besserer family to glaze the small chapel named after them.

To match the scale of the building, the little windows of Bible scenes in the Besserer Chapel possess a strange mixture of sophistication and innocence. For instance, Acker's Noah window shows the old man emerging from a huge chimney-like opening in the dolls-house roof of the ark, while his children stare longingly from windows in the ship's superstructure.

Samson and the lion; Church of St Etienne, Mulhouse, Alsace, France.

Florence Cathedral

Florence Cathedral, another world-renowned example of church architecture, famous for its great dome designed by the local architect, Filippo Brunelleschi, also houses a magnificent gallery of stained glass, by Italian artists of considerable note. Although work on the cathedral commenced in 1300, progress in its construction was slow, due to war, civil strife and the power of the local guilds. The vast cupola was not put in place until late in the fifteenth century, when Brunelleschi solved the peculiar technical problems associated with such an enterprise.

The cathedral has eleven 'eye' windows, ten of them designed by major fifteenth-century artists — Ghiberti, Donatello, Del Castagno and Uccello. Unlike the great rose windows of Gothic cathedrals, these eye windows were uninterrupted by stone tracery, and allowed the artist to design the entire circle in glass, divided only by horizontal and vertical metal bars.

Uccello's eye windows, depicting the Nativity and the Resurrection, are outstandingly beautiful, and reflect his ability to introduce naturalism to biblical subjects. The eye window by Andrea del Castagno depicts Christ being lifted down from the cross. Ghiberti was responsible for three of the eye windows: he depicted the Ascension; the Prayer in the Garden; and the Presentation in the Temple. He also designed at least eleven of the windows in the apse and chapels of the cathedral; these windows are notable for their rich colouring and bold designs.

The artists responsible for these windows were remarkably versatile in their gifts. Lorenzo Ghiberti was also a goldsmith, bronze-worker, sculptor, painter and architect; Donatello was the father of modern sculpture; Paolo Uccello and Andrea del Castagno, among their many other accomplishments, also created splendid painted frescoes for the cathedral.

Great Malvern Priory Church

But in medieval England it was not only the great cathedrals that boasted rich collections of stained glass. Sometimes the ordinary parish church could be equally splendidly endowed. The Priory Church of Great Malvern, Worcestershire, England, provides a fine example. This church was rebuilt in 1460; soon after this date all forty windows of the building were filled with stained glass, a good proportion of which has survived down to present times.

Dr Tim Dowley

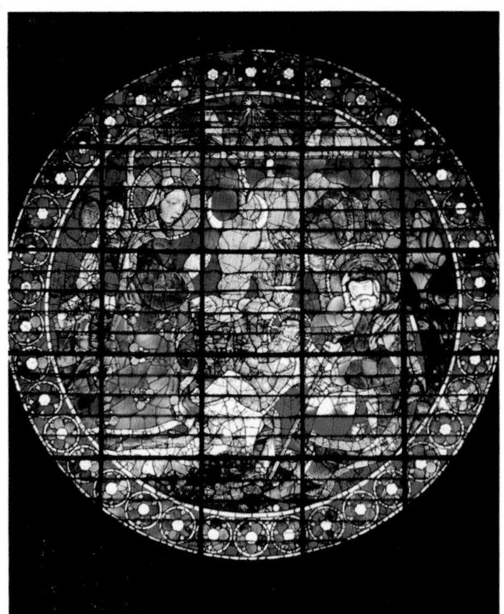

The Nativity; Lunette by Paolo Uccello in the dome of Florence Cathedral, Italy; 1443/4.

The West End of Chartres Cathedral.

The West Rose Window and 'Gallery of Kings', exterior of Chartres Cathedral, France.

Photographing the Glass

We started photographing stained glass in 1971, the results culminating in our magnum opus *Stained Glass* (Mitchell Beazley, 1976). We then worked for seven seasons photographing all the stained glass and sculpture of Chartres Cathedral. Our long-term ambition has been one day to illustrate the Bible in stained glass, an ambition which is achieved with this book. We hope the book will give as much pleasure to you, the reader, as we had while we were taking the photographs. We would like to thank everyone who has been so kind and helpful in arranging permission to photograph the glass, and in helping to hire scaffolding, as we have undertaken this huge project.

In achieving a good photograph of stained glass, it is essential to get as close to the window as possible, which of course entails scaffolding, ladders (and even, in the case of Cologne Cathedral, a fireman's ladder!). On ladders, we use a Sinar clamp with extension rods, since rigidity is essential, with the Pentax 6x7cm body plus lens weighing as much as eight pounds. In addition, we use rope as a fail-safe measure, should anything give way.

Exposures vary between one and ten seconds, though we don't use a release cable, but grasp the camera firmly, breath held in, simultaneously pressing the release button with the thumb. The most valuable piece of equipment for stained glass photography is the Asahi Spotmeter, which gives a one-degree angle; through-the-lens metering is useless for this work since it gives a false reading. When working from scaffolding, we use either a Bilora or Kennet tripod with a Linhof head. We employ a range of lenses: 55mm, 75mm shift (the ability to shift the lens laterally or horizontally is invaluable, since it saves having to move the scaffolding a few inches or feet), 105mm, 135mm, 200mm, 300mm and 400mm. We use the 400mm for shooting a detail in a rose window from the triforium or clerestory opposite.

In smaller churches we place 4′ 6″ wooden planks across the tops of the pews and balance the tripod and step-ladder on them, having of course first obtained the necessary permission. We are always very careful to ensure that at no time during our photographic sessions is there any sense of irreverence.

We never photograph windows with direct sunlight coming through; in fact a dull day is preferable, and thick fog ideal! Trees can cast unwanted shadows across a window, or show green through the glass. In case of such difficulties, Laura holds up outside the window a white sheet on a pair of ten-foot canes (an operation only possible in small churches!). In Spain, where stained glass windows can often be opened, we have worked on roof-tops in temperatures as high as 49°C (120°F), shooting through the open window to the window on the opposite side of the nave.

We always use Ektachrome film, formerly 64ASA, now 100ASA. We use slow film, because 200ASA and 400ASA Ektachrome tends to be too blue. Laura has recorded the date, time, place, subject, lens, aperture, speed and weather conditions for every single shot of stained glass we have taken. This means we can return to any location to re-photograph a window which has been cleaned or restored, and know exactly at what time of day it has to be re-shot.

Sonia Halliday

A nineteenth-century window showing the seventeenth-century restoration of the building, in the South Choir Aisle of Lichfield Cathedral, Staffordshire, England.

The authors photographing some of the stained glass at Lichfield Cathedral.

Index

Page numbers in italics refer to full-page illustrations.

INDEX OF PLACES WHERE THE STAINED GLASS ILLUSTRATED IS FOUND

General Index